Humanist Geography

Humanist Geography

An Individual's Search for Meaning
by Yi-Fu Tuan

George F. Thompson Publishing

for John Perry and Jared Shlaes

Contents

Acknowledgments

————————

I MARKED MY EIGHTIETH BIRTHDAY on December 5, 2010, at my stepsister's home in California. About twenty-five people, spanning three generations, were present, including two former students from the University of Wisconsin-Madison. Contributing greatly to the liveliness of the occasion were the offspring of my nieces and nephew and the Kern children: Andrew (age twelve), Benjamin (ten), and Abigail (five). The older of the three—the two boys—claimed me to be their grandfather. It wasn't an empty claim, for they clinched it with phone calls and long letters. Yet we had not met prior to my birthday party, nor had I previously met their parents. So how come?

It all came about through a school teacher by the name of John Perry, my pen pal of many years. He taught the children's father at a private school in Connecticut and persuaded me to write a book on education that could benefit children everywhere. That, actually, is how *Humanist Geography* got started, and that is why the book contains several early chapters on education. So thank you, John. At my age and never having married, it is a miracle to be a grandfather!

I also extend heartfelt thanks to another long-time friend, Jared Shlaes, of Chicago, for his unwavering support after first reading *Segmented Worlds and Self* nearly thirty years ago, and to all those on the GFT Team who were such an integral part of making this book possible: George F. Thompson, editor and publisher; David Skolkin, book designer and art director; Carmen Rose Shenk and Stephanie Lichner, editorial assistants; Purna Makaram, manuscript editor; and Alison Drew Hunt, indexer. J. Nicholas Eritrikin, Dominic Pacyga, Paul F. Starrs, and Denis Wood provided excellent editorial advice during important stages in the manuscript's evolution into a book, and Richard Misrach graciously allowed us to reproduce two photographs from his renowned "On the Beach" series that perfectly complement a main thrust of humanism in this book: the individual versus the group.

Thank you, one and all!

Humanist Geography

To Be Human

———————

I TAUGHT HUMANIST GEOGRAPHY for nearly forty years. On the first day of class I would say to some fifty students. "I hope you realize that you are taking a practical course. By 'practical' I mean encountering new knowledge and ways of thinking that will be of use to you."

The students would look puzzled, for they already knew, either through hearsay or through having read something I wrote, that I was in no way an applied or practical geographer nor an expert on maps or on GIS (geographic information science), knowledge of which would give them employable skills. In any case, the very word "humanist" in the course title gave it away as impractical. I then would explain:

> Let's say that our life span is the biblical "three-score and ten"; that is, seventy years. Seventy years translate into approximately 600,000 hours. Subtract a third of that time for sleep, and we have 400,000 hours left to do what we need or like to do. Now, if we work full-time for fifty years, we will have spent something like 150,000 hours earning our daily bread; 250,000 hours remain during which we live and live it up: eat, socialize, go to the movies, watch television, play golf, potter around, daydream.[1] A practical course in college can be of use to us in the working life but impractical for the rest. Humanist geography, by contrast, is impractical for the working life but practical for the days, hours, and half-hours that are our own, when we are free. How so? It empowers us to be engaged productively with certain questions that are incumbent upon us as thinking men and women to raise—and to raise them with a sense of urgency, for our time on Earth as individuals is the briefest. The questions are: "What is it—what does it mean—to be human? More specifically, what does being human mean for me?"

So stated, these questions are just the sort that can seem impractical and irrelevant to people who, for all their natural curiosity, are put off by excessive abstraction. Humanist geography can bring the questions closer to Earth. But what is humanist geography? The words "humanist" and "geography" themselves suggest an answer. Insofar as I am a humanist, I focus on the individual—individualism being a child of humanism. Insofar as I am a geographer, I focus on community and place—the social and material dimensions of living. The large abstract questions concerning life and its meaning will still be raised but grounded in the facts of ordinary existence.

The two components of humanist geography—the individual and one's community—are somewhat at odds with each other. To the extent that I play up the individual, I play down community and vice versa. Another well-known contraposed pair follows from the fact that humans form groups at different scales. At one end of the scale is the local and communal; at the other end is the worldwide and cosmopolitan. The first of the pair—the local and the communal—produces a strong sense of group self and an "us vs. them" mentality that, historically, has often led to conflict. On the positive side, it promotes neighborliness within the group and encourages cultural diversity overall, because each group is likely to have its own distinctive customs and products. The second of the pair—the world of cosmopolites—is made up of first-person singulars (the "I"s or individuals) who freely associate; their challenge lies in sustaining neighborly commitment and care. Additionally, while cosmopolitanism promotes individual excellence and the highest level of achievement, it also has the effect, though unwittingly, of trampling on local culture. Again, to the extent that I play up the local and the communal, I play down cosmopolitanism and the world and vice versa.

Of the pair's alternatives, which is favored today? Among social workers and activists, community and cultural diversity are decidedly favored over individualism and cosmopolitanism. To them and, increasingly, to the general public, the word "community" evokes a warm, positive feeling. Sociologist Raymond Williams (1921–1988) notes that, "unlike all other terms of social organization (state, nation, society, etc.), it seems never to be used unfavorably."[2] The same can be said of cultural diversity. To speak well of it at once puts one on the side of angels. By contrast, individualism—not long ago the pride of Western civilization—is more and more often seen in a negative light. When the word and its cognates (individual, individuality) come up, self-centeredness—a commitment to personal success at the expense of community—is implied. Cosmopolitanism has also lost ground in public esteem. Its aspiration toward intellectual and artistic excellence smacks of elitism, and its products, both good and bad, are seen to smother native talents and cultures.[3]

To effect a better balance between the alternatives, I offer a favorable view of the individual and cosmopolitan society, and I begin by asking, "What are the advantages and disadvantages for me in social groups of varying size and complexity?" My answer goes something like this: in a small and close-knit community, I am assured of human warmth—of being provided with chicken soup when I have a bad cold. On the other hand, it isolates me from the riches of the world and doesn't encourage me to grow to my full potential. In a cosmopolitan society, I am free to be myself and to develop my talents, whatever these are, with the help of its numerous amenities. But I won't know my neighbor and cannot count on chicken soup. Community has the advantage of being egalitarian: no one lords over another in wealth or social prestige. Cosmopolitan society is, by its nature, hierarchical, with many pyramids of excellence in which one can hope to rise. Whether I can rise to my full potential depends, however, on my social position and on the economic advantages I have inherited. In a cosmopolitan society, therefore, issues of justice and injustice, equality and inequality, loom large.

Why, one might ask, the fuss about a human individual in the first place? What, in the end, does a handful of dust—an individual's ultimate fate—matter? Humanism has no adequate response; or, rather, to the extent that it has, it draws on an older way of thinking called religion. Religious thinking at its best is not, therefore, a relic that humanism has to outgrow. Quite the contrary: religious thinking both undergirds and completes humanist thinking. It is humanist thinking that dares to push imagination to the edge of fantasy.

These views on humanism are not universally shared. Secular humanists, or rationalists, rule out a priori any input from religious and theological scholarship. I consider the exclusion regrettable, for it narrows the scope of inquiry and offends the spirit of humanism, which was and is to open up and not to close off.

From what I have said thus far, it is clear that I have certain predilections. I like to think these are grounded on facts and reason, but surely they reflect my social and educational background, all the more so since humanist geography, unlike physical or economic geography, has no set topics established by general consensus. The topics that I explore in this book are also taken up by other humanist geographers, though not all of them and not all to the same degree. Hence, the need for me to add a subtitle, indicating the personal nature of this work: "An Individual's Search for Meaning."

The subtitle calls for a sketch of my childhood and youth, in Part I, with special emphasis on education, for it was during this early period of my life that the topics I now raise first emerged. Naturally, I lacked the words for them then. Decades had to pass before I could tentatively articulate life's meaning. My hope is that whoever reads the book will be tempted to make a similar effort, not necessarily in writing—much less in the form of a book—but rather in long, reflective pauses when he or she is not swamped by the cares and stresses of the world.

PART I

Getting Educated

CHAPTER 1

Chongqing

B ETWEEN AGES SEVEN AND TEN (1938–1941) I attended a one-room school in war-ravaged Chongqing that was established in 1938 by my father and his friends. They were prompted to do so because no elementary school existed in the neighborhood and their children were too young to be admitted to Nankai, the famous middle school. Nankai's headmaster encouraged our parents. He not only gave them permission to use his school's name, but also provided a room next to Nankai's electricity generating station. So what did I learn in that one room? No doubt arithmetic, but I don't remember how I learnt it, perhaps because it was taught in the conventional way. I do remember reading and writing, particularly reading. We children read stories drawn from both Chinese and Western sources.

Chinese stories encouraged studiousness, filial piety, and patriotism. Seventy years later, I can still remember some of them.

One story tells of a village boy who worked on the farm during the day and so could study only at night. The problem there was that his family couldn't afford even a candle. So the boy caught fireflies, put them in a gauze net, and read by their light. With this story, we children were encouraged to admire not only the desire to learn, but also the ingenuity to find the means. We were not to regard poverty as an insurmountable barrier.

The second story teaches filial piety and is Chinese to the core. A woman, extremely poor, was dying for lack of nourishment. (Note the recurrent theme of poverty.) Her son cut a slice of flesh from his arm and used it to make soup for his mother. A non-Chinese reader might be shocked by the violence, but, as a Chinese child steeped in the culture, I took it in stride.

The third story I remember is a lesson in patriotism. A hero to all Chinese is the Song general Yue Fei (1113–1142) who fought to prevent northern tribes from invading what remained of the Song empire. A picture in the book shows the general kneeling besides his mother. On his bare back, the mother wrote, "*Huan wo ho shan*" (Return to us our rivers and mountains). Given the fact that the China of my childhood was encircled by Japanese armies and fighting for its life, I am surprised that more such patriotic stories were not included in our reader. It could be that our parents and teachers, knowing how nationalistic fervor could get out of hand and leave a permanent mark at our impressionable age, restrained themselves.

My father and his friends attended university together. After graduation, they left China for graduate studies in Europe and the United States (that is, America.) When they returned home, either to teach or to take up positions in the government, they formed a small core of cosmopolites who, when they met, engaged in the liveliest conversation. On calm summer evenings, sitting outdoors to cool off, one of them might look up at the night sky and point to Orion. That could trigger a lively exchange on astronomy—not only on the science, but also on Greek mythology, which, in turn, raised the question, "How come we Chinese didn't mythologize the stars?" Another friend might mention a new Hollywood movie in town, an offhand remark that could trigger a discussion of Yuan-dynasty (1279–1368) drama and whether it lent itself to filming. Educational policy? A Confucianist and an admirer of John Dewey's (1859–1952) philosophy of education might debate the merit and demerit of rote learning. To a nine-year-old boy, hearing all of this excited talk under a ceiling of stars was an unforgettable treat.

Given my father and his cohort's post-graduate education in the West, it is understandable that several of the stories we children read were Western: we read about the apple that fell on Isaac Newton (1642–1727), the kite that Benjamin Franklin (1706–1790) flew in a storm to tap electricity, and the absentmindedness of young James Watts (1736–1819). But I believe there was a more conscious reason: namely, our parents wanted us to be daring intellectually, and it would seem they couldn't come up with suitable Chinese tales for that purpose. The apple that fell on Newton allowed our teacher to introduce us to gravity and the solar system, Franklin's kite flying opened up the topic of electricity. But what mattered to us more in the long run was that the stories encouraged unconventional thinking and behavior. Singed into our young brain was the idea that it might be better to daydream under an apple tree than grind out additions and subtractions at home, that doing science was worth risking electrocution in a storm.

My favorite story concerns young James Watts, the future inventor of the steam engine. It is said that he often sat alone and stared into space, thinking. His mother, wanting him to be more practical, assigned him a job, which was to time the cooking of an egg. "Here is the egg," she said. "Put it into the boiling water. And here is a watch. Be sure to take the egg out before two minutes are up." Two minutes later, Watts's mother returned. She peered into the boiling water and found, to her horror, her watch. Her son, meanwhile, was staring quizzically at the egg in his hand. Were the grown-ups telling us that it was all right to boil mother's watch if the steam engine lay in the future?

Chinese stories tend to emphasize morality; Western ones, mental curiosity and imagination. A story that addresses both is *The Happy Prince* (1888) by Oscar Wilde (1854–1900). Again, I am impressed by our parents' and teachers' acumen. They selected this tale to include in our reader, because they felt that Chinese ones tended to confine the doing of good to family members and neighbors who could reciprocate and left out strangers who could not. Most Western tales are also defective in that they end unrealistically in marriage and living happily thereafter. The ethic of *The Happy Prince* is of a higher order, universalist in its mingling of Buddhist compassion and Christian salvation and universalist in its transcendence of mere local give-and-take and of easy optimism. The story ends in cruel death for both the prince and the swallow, a touch of realism that may well win a nod from the perceptive young reader. It may also leave him with the conviction that the prince and the swallow, in their willingness to die for strangers in desperate need, have done absolutely the right thing. And that absolute rightness, a rare but real possibility in life, makes for joy.

As for the education of our aesthetic sensibility, I don't remember lessons in drawing or painting, as are common in Western schools. Perhaps there was less need for art classes in China, because calligraphy served that purpose. Learning to write, a chore for the child, is fun when its preliminaries include ink-making. I remember taking out my ink tablet and stone slab from my satchel, pouring a smidgin of water on the slab, and grinding away to produce a black paste, smearing my fingers in the process. Writing with a brush can be fun, too, and magical in that the thickness and slant of a line, the looseness or compactness of the completed character, enrich the word's meaning.

Young bodies need exercise. We didn't have competitive sports if only because we were too few to form teams. And I can't remember that we ever did physical exercises of the kind one so often finds in today's China. Being children, we did play games, such as rope skipping, hide-and-seek, treasure hunt, or among boys, good-natured fighting.

One game stands out in my memory. It is called chicken-and-hawk, and I believe that variants of it are played by children all over the world. In the game, one child pretends to be the mother hen. Lined up behind her are the chicks. The hawk attempts to catch a chick. The mother does her best to prevent it by spreading her wings and turning this way and that with the chicks swinging wildly behind her.

In the role of a chick, I felt vulnerable and shrieked with excitement as I dodged the predatory hawk. In the next game, I may have taken on the role of the protective mother hen and then that of the predatory hawk. The game teaches children that their moods and behavior are not consistent, as robots' are, and that, at times, they can feel vulnerable and scared, at other times protective and nurturing or even aggressive and predatory.

Another game, invented by the philosopher Ludwig Wittgenstein (1889–1951), is likewise both enjoyable and educational. I can imagine our school adopting it when the time comes for the children to learn about the solar system. The usual method has the teacher standing behind a model and telling the class about the gravitational forces that keep the moon, earth, and sun moving around one another. This approach, to Wittgenstein, is much too passive. At the end of the demonstration the children will still not have any *feel* for gravitational force. To acquire that feel Wittgenstein recommends a game that will certainly appeal to children. On the playground let the boy be the sun, moving slowly in one direction. Let a girl be Earth: her assignment is to run around the boy who is the sun. Let another girl be the moon: her assignment is the most demanding of all, for she has to dash around Earth as Earth runs around the sun and as the sun itself moves outward in an expanding universe. After a while, the boy and girls switch roles so that each can know what it is like to be a particular heavenly body.[1]

These two games refer to the external world—society in the one case and the solar system in the other. Games that have no such reference do not appeal to me. I avoid them because they all seem to start with a set of arbitrary rules, which those who wish to play simply have to accept. Why do two minuses make a plus? I wondered. Our teacher never explained. Children who like math also like games. They do not object to a game's rules, since within their constraints they can find ingenious means to triumph over their opponent. Satisfaction lies in finding these means and in winning and not in touching base with something "out there" called the real world.

Arithmetic and geometry do, of course, touch base with the real world. An ability to add, subtract, divide, and multiply gives one an immediate sense of control over objects, whether they be apples or coins. And geometry has its origin in the need to find the exact shape and size of fields, which are clearly of interest to farmers and landowners. Elementary schools all over the world treat arithmetic and geometry as practical subjects. They are right to do so, as they are right to insist that reading and writing at a high level of competence are crucial to success in a literate society. But, if these school subjects and skills were the only gains, my childhood education would not be worth reporting. There was something more, almost magical, that I attribute to the stories. Most of them simply offered information; significantly, I remember none of the information they offered. A few were entertaining and inspirational; they continue to be both as I recollect them in memory. One, *The Happy Prince*, introduced me to another world of transcendant charity that inspires me.

CHAPTER 2

Sydney

———

MIDDLE-SCHOOL AND MOST OF MY HIGH-SCHOOL YEARS (1942–1946) were spent in Sydney, Australia. The school, Cranbrook, was a good one. My brothers and I didn't know a word of English when we entered, which was a daunting experience, and it didn't help when beefy Australian boys danced around us, chanting a racist ditty. Were we frightened, humiliated, demoralized? No. Well, perhaps I was a little frightened but certainly not humiliated or demoralized. How could this be? Racist taunting is now unacceptable—correctly so, but I doubt that it has the power to set back its victim academically, as is the current belief.

My brothers and I were immune to racist taunting for two reasons. First, we learned in early childhood that China was a civilization surrounded by barbarians. Australian boys, jumping and hooting, unwittingly played that role. Far from demoralizing us, they confirmed our sense of civilizational superiority. The second reason was the cosmopolitan education we received in that one-room school. Young children distinguish between good people and bad people, but, unless explicitly taught, they do not distinguish between foreigner and native. As an eight-year-old I knew that Yue Fei was Chinese, but I never thought of Newton, Franklin, and Watts as foreigners. They all exuded the glamor of exceptional talent, which made me want to emulate them. Having these figures as my role models and never once questioning that I had a right to them was immensely confidence building.

Why can't all children start their education with a universalist or cosmopolitan fare? We seem to have forgotten that children are naturally drawn to the cosmopolitan and the exotic. By the time American children reach elementary school, they are more likely to be thrilled by Egyptian pyramids and the Great Wall of China than by the local town hall and water tower, more by dinosaurs than by cows. Adults strive to ensure that their children grow up chauvinistic, for they see it as a way to maintain a strong sense of community. It goes without saying that a strong sense of community is necessary to the demands of livelihood and survival, but these do not concern children. They are at an age—perhaps the only time in their life—when they are true intellectuals, and they should be encouraged to be such, as I was in that one-room school.

My childhood gave me a taste of cosmopolitanism. What experiences and revelations came my way in my Australian childhood? Three are worth mentioning. One is an awareness of natural beauty. As a child in Chongqing I didn't see nature as a separate category, perhaps because we lived in the countryside. Playing among the terraced rice fields, clambering from one level to the next, I was too absorbed in the game and in my bodily exertions to pause and heed my environment. Our parents occasionally took my brothers, sister, and me to a temple on top of a nearby mountain. I enjoyed the outing, the freshness of the air, and the physical exertion, which made the vegetarian meal at the temple heavenly, but the mountain itself barely registered. It was in Australia, during a trip to the Three Sisters—three towering pinnacles carved out of a sweeping escarpment about fifty miles from Sydney—that made me pause, I believe for the first time, to wonder at nature's scale and unfathomable otherness.

The second new awareness was of social class. What I had taken for granted as natural, in the order of things, became problematic. Between 1942 and 1946, father was the Chinese consul-general in Sydney. His job was to look after the Chinese community, mostly small businessmen, and see to it that they were treated fairly by Australians. I soon noticed the deference that these businessmen paid my father and his family. As the resident Chinese official father had many callers—the local Chinese who needed his help and VIPs from China. The locals gave father presents from time to time, which I regarded as tokens of their appreciation for his help beyond the call of duty. Father, for his part, gave presents to the VIPs, the value of which varied with the recipient's rank. Such giving struck me as obsequious. When I questioned father, the answer he gave was a neat encapsulation of the teaching of modern sociology, grounded ultimately on relationships of power. And so, in striking contrast with my first real encounter with nature, which gave me reason to look forward to more such encounters, my first understanding of the real nature of society made me view my future entry into it with distaste.

The third awareness was religious. For the first time I toyed with the idea of another reality that ran parallel with, and periodically intruded upon, the one I had always known. Cranbrook School has a Church of England foundation. Each week, we attended chapel. Not having been raised a Christian and not knowing much English, the service was baffling to my brothers and me. One day, the form master called us into his office, lined us up in from of him, and proceeded to tell us about Jesus, the son of God, the miracles he performed, and what he said in his Sermon on the Mount (Matthew 5–7). I was taken aback that our teacher, a figure of authority, could tell us with a straight face about a man who walked on water, healed the blind, and raised the dead. And I was even more astonished to be told that, in the kingdom of God, there will be a reversal of norms such that the first will be last, and the last first, the rich are burdened by their wealth and the poor blessed by their poverty. As for entering the heavenly kingdom, children have a better chance than learned adults.

CHAPTER 3

Oxford

_____

"WHAT ABOUT OXFORD?" Oxford meant much to me, more for the opportunities to learn and to think in an atmosphere of calm beauty than for new revelations. To go to Oxford I had to declare a major or "read a subject," as the Brits say. I declared mine to be geography, which may seem surprising given my romantic and philosophical inclinations. At age sixteen I already knew that, despite the obvious draw of philosophy, I would find it too abstract. I didn't want to reach the end of life with only doubt and uncertainty as my acquisitions. I needed the reassurance of empirical facts, and no field of study was to me more empirically grounded and down-to-Earth than geography. Since where and why people make a living in different parts of the world was and still is the core of the discipline, I would begin with the economics of livelihood and then move on to non-economic desires and aspirations, to what human beings, as individuals and in a group, can potentially be.

Unfortunately, human geography at Oxford in the period after World War II was rather dry. I forced myself to learn as much as I could, applying to geography the discipline I acquired studying dull school subjects at Cranbrook. Meanwhile, the Oxford system, which did not require students to take set courses or be tested except at the end of three years, encouraged them to read widely, attend public lectures on all sorts of subjects, and, above all, talk to one another in small gatherings until dawn breaks or until they ran out of shillings to put in the gas meter. Without knowing it I acquired a well-rounded, if undisciplined, liberal arts education.

Oxford in my years there (1948–1951) was experiencing a religious revival. But how misleading the words "religious revival" and, for that matter, "religion" can be! Today, they call to mind a fundamentalist ethos that favors a literal reading of *The Holy Bible*, evangelical fervor, and devotion to family values. Religious revival in my time at Oxford was on quite another plane—pious and learned. We drew inspiration not only from Christian writers, such as G. K. Chesterton (1874–1936), C. S. Lewis (1888–1965), and T. S. Eliot (1888–1965), but also from non-religious Existentialist philosophers, such as Martin Heidegger

(1889–1976), Jean-Paul Sartre (1905–1980), and Albert Camus (1913–1960). Our questions were hardly original. What is the meaning of life? Is suicide absurd? Is there life beyond death, and how can it be imagined other than through the usual bland stereotypes? How is human goodness manifest? And does goodness matter beyond what is necessary to ensure cooperation and group survival? Perhaps, in the end, what we asked, as serious young people, was simply, "What is the best way for us to lead the only life we have?"

In American schools and colleges, no effort is made to offer a course that addresses questions of this kind. Philosophy is not taught in secondary schools. It is taught in colleges and universities but routinely as capsules of philosophical thought or, at the other extreme, as a highly technical subject for specialists. American public schools are forbidden to offer religion in their curriculum except as a survey of religious practices—the corn dance, ancestor worship, Passover, Holy Communion, and so on. Religion thus turns into sociology or cultural anthropology and carries no hint of transcendence—of a morality that goes beyond custom or of human life that goes beyond bio-social life.

CHAPTER 4

Berkeley

—————————

THREE INFLUENCES AFFECTED MY OUTLOOK ON LIFE and world in the next stage of my education, which was to take place at the University of California at Berkeley. Actually, the first of these came while I was still on my way there. As the train crossed the Great Plains and the intermontane deserts I felt an expansion of spirit I had not quite known earlier. What appealed to me were the clarity, simplicity, and openness of the landscapes. Although I didn't know it at the time, I now see that these expansive natural features answered a deep psychological need in me. I now also see why the city—the ideal cosmic city—makes me want to sing that charming villages and colorful folk customs do not. Strange as it may sound, I am not only more buoyed up, but even more at ease in a city than I can ever be in a small town or village.

At Berkeley, I at last found the sort of intellectual effervescence in human geography that I had hoped for at Oxford but didn't find. Carl Sauer (1887–1975), who established Berkeley's department of geography in 1923, remained its guiding light, even though he was on the verge of retirement. In his seminars, graduate students were encouraged to address "man's role in changing the face of the earth." Sauer was pessimistic about man's stewardship and saw more abuse than wise use in the so-called civilized societies. He had little good to say about the city as such and seldom referred to it, except critically, in his course on cultural geography. In striking contrast, he enthused over simple folks, their cultures and customs, their nurturing ways with the earth.

I found myself in a curious position. I greatly admired the far-ranging intellect of Carl Sauer yet couldn't embrace his love of folk, his romantic view of nature, if only because he himself lived the high style of a city man. I wrote a term paper for him in which I praised the city—I had San Francisco in mind—and declared my belief in progress. In other words, I, twenty-one years old and a first-year graduate student, deliberately went counter to the Great Man's views and values. The end of my career? Far from it. Sauer gave me an A, no doubt amused by my boldness, a trait he wished to encourage in his students.

The third influence came my way at Berkeley, not from the geography department or even from the university but from society at large. The tail end of my graduate student years (1951–1957) coincided with the beginning of America's civil rights movement. Even as a child I rebelled against the notion that power ruled the world. When I first encountered Christianity at Cranbrook School in Sydney, it understandably appealed to me, if only because it says that love moves the stars, not brute force. Like every idealistic young person, I was all for civil rights and social justice, but, unlike my peers, I was and am keenly aware of irreducible injustices that remain even in a caring society. What can civil rights and social welfare do for injustices of the past or for inequalities of the present that are grounded in biology and accidents of birth? My problem, I now realize, is that, as a humanist, I see individuals rather than groups, and it is glaringly obvious to me that gifts and opportunities in individuals differ widely.

CHAPTER 5

Humanism, Temporal Direction, and Progress

F ROM MY EARLIEST YEARS IN CHINA to my current life in Madison, Wisconsin, I have retained a streak of optimism throughout my life, despite periodic assaults by dark thoughts. One manifestation of my optimism is a sympathy for the idea of progress, to which I return again and again, reluctant to give it up even in the face of contrary evidence. What ultimately holds me in thrall may well be just a temperamental bias in favor of directional time. I say this because some of my other favorite words—development, growth, and transcendence—also imply directional time.

There is nothing extraordinary in this bias. Life itself is directional and progressive. Children grow up. They mature physically and mentally. In the course of time, they reach a certain level of intellectual understanding. That level is defined by society. Once reached, men and women are discouraged from going further. Progress, considered good in all the prior stages of their upbringing, comes to a stop. To go beyond is deemed reprehensible, a threat to society's cohesion and stability.

Perhaps, for this reason, societies in the past have seldom entertained the idea of directional time and progress. Pre-literate peoples, for example, take for granted that their customs and practices are not so much products of their ingenuity, improved over time, as handed down to them by deities, shamans, and ancestral heroes. Their obligation is to maintain whatever harmony there is through traditional customs and practices. The idea that they can or ought to be improved is alien and even sacrilegious.

Civilized people lived in architectural piles that obviously couldn't have been built in a day. Unlike a small village, the city speaks loud and clear of history, of being the terminus of a long, cumulative process. Yet the civilized, too, may see their world not as the result of an upward climb but as the last stage of a long decline. The Greeks, who postulated four ages—gold, silver, bronze, and iron—saw theirs as iron, the most humble of the four. The Chinese also postulated a golden age in the past—one ruled by wise kings. Not progress but restoration was the Chinese ideal. It is only in the West, and only from the eighteenth century onward, that the idea of society moving ever "forward and upward" firmly took hold. Notwithstanding its many critics during the last hundred years or so, the idea still underlies much Western thought.

Humanism has contributed to progress in its promotion of the autonomous individual. A truly good community is, in its eyes, one in which each member has enough self-confidence to think and recollect alone. Thinking and recollecting alone recharges the self and enhances self-knowledge. The self, thus recharged and thus better known, is empowered to engage others in fruitful conversation. Fruitful conversation leads to friendship, increased knowledge, and the taking up of joint projects that promote the common good. The common good, thus enriched, provides a milieu in which individuals can rise to a still higher level of well-being and achievement. What I am describing is a benign circle. Curious that we often hear of the vicious circle but seldom—if ever—of the benign circle. Yet it must be of fairly common occurrence, for otherwise human society would have stagnated or turned hellish.

It should be clear by now that a generally positive outlook informs my account of humanist geography in the pages to follow. I don't want to give readers the impression, however, that I am about to lead them on a rosy tour of human reality. To forestall that possibility, before I reach those parts of the book that do revel in human potential and achievements, I will establish my credentials for sobriety and even hard-headedness by offering, first, a quasi-sociological account of self, community, and world and, then, a bareknuckled account of human frailties and evil.

PART II

Self, Community, and World

CHAPTER 6

Isolated Selves and Bonding

INDIVIDUAL DIFFERENCES

AN EGREGIOUS GAP IN EDUCATION programs is the awareness of how human beings, more than any other animal species, differ from one another. I myself, for all my interest in people and their ways, am guilty of this neglect. My excuse is that my profession as a teacher means that I live among healthy youngsters who all look much alike, who all have roughly the same bodily shape and the same bright shining faces, who stand, slouch in the chair, and move about in much the same way. The shock comes when I visit a large city, such as Chicago, and am confronted by an extraordinary range of human types. I can believe that the slim young woman, the man built like a sumo wrestler, the unsteady toddler, the shuffling old man, the teenager on his skateboard, the rod-straight marine, the bent beggar, the bearded six-foot-two and the mustachioed four-foot-six, the swarthy and the pale, all belong to the same species only because they are all clothed. Naked, and I would have thought I had strayed into a zoo.

Humans stand out as individuals. We see their differences, but even more remarkable are the differences we don't see—those under the skin. The size and shape of stomachs vary far more than do the size and shape of noses and mouths. If noses vary proportionately to stomachs, some would look like cucumbers, others like pumpkins. A hand with six fingers is considered abnormal; not so, however, the pipes that branch from the aorta above the heart, which number from one to six. Individuals equipped with a narrow esophagus have a difficult time swallowing pills; at the opposite extreme, those well favored may accidentally ingest a whole set of false teeth.

The perceptual senses differ much in scope and degree of sensitivity, even among individuals considered normal. Ears vary significantly in their receptiveness to sound frequencies; a range that is barely registered by some may be vividly registered by others. When pitch sensitivity is combined with other capabilities of hearing, people's daily lives are differentially affected, in matters such as tolerance of the level and kind of noise, ability to grasp certain words in speech, and appreciation of music. Eye tests reveal unique strengths and weaknesses. Differences in peripheral vision, for example, are large enough to affect competence in sports, driving cars, flying airplanes, and perhaps even in the ease and speed of reading. Color vision is a species trait. Within that general capacity are wide variations in sensitivity to shades of color and to a color's richness. "Is the redness of the rose the same to you as to me?" lovers may wonder as, hand in hand, they stroll through a garden. But the question is not merely philosophical; it is also neurological, for it depends, in part, on the number of pigment genes on the eye's X chromosomes.[1]

Most remarkable of all are the differences in the human brain. Every feature that has been measured shows surprising diversity. The brain makes every individual truly unique. A wizard at chess may not be good at algebra. Excellence in one branch of mathematics does not guarantee high performance in another. The talented French mathematician Jacques Hadamard (1865–1963) admits that he has difficulty mastering Lie group: it is as though his mental energy for that speciality is exhausted in attaining mere competence. Some people are very verbal, but there, too, the talent may show itself in one area rather than in another—for example, in poetry rather than in prose. Can this be attributed to genes? We do know that, as a result of a defective gene, some individuals have difficulty forming plurals, although in other respects they speak and write normally.

One consequence of human biological uniqueness is that a person often feels slightly out of step with other persons, including ones who are closest by virtue of blood or affection—still eating when others have finished, feeling cold when others complain of heat, unable to catch the meaning of a sentence when others nod, and so on through the course of an ordinary day. Such reminders of disconnectedness are routinely suppressed in the interest of commonality— of sustaining a sense of belonging. Sense of belonging must be especially deep in the family to ensure its survival and reproductive success. Members need to feel that they are "one." They are not, however, "one": distinguished from one another by age, sex, and temperament, their perception, emotion, and understanding have less in common than any other group of comparable size, be they businessmen, college students, Wal-Mart moms, or even any group arbitrarily selected from a city's crowded sidewalk.

Years ago, I attended a party in honor of a girl's first birthday. Her father, whom I knew well, was a graduate student in the university where I taught. The small apartment was packed with people: the little girl and her older brother, their parents and grandparents, other graduate students, and a few family friends like me. The single candle on the cake was extinguished with parental help, the cake was cut and distributed, and then we dispersed. Some went to the kitchen to do the washing up, while others stood about in the living room or found comfortable chairs to sit on. The grandparents looked relaxed and drowsy; the graduate students talked with animation; the little boy rushed around on his tricycle, almost bumping into his sister, who was beginning to act up and clearly needed her afternoon nap.

At first, I simply wallowed in this cozy little world. Then, as I looked about me, I realized that we at the party were individuals who barely communicated with one another. The age difference between the boy and his sister made mutual understanding nearly impossible; the grandfather woke up to make a comment on the weather to which no one heeded; our host was drying dishes with his wife, but his mind seemed elsewhere; the other graduate students were arguing. Each at the party was a unique being locked into his or her separate reality. Yet that was not how we felt. That was not how *I* felt until my critical faculties were stirred.

Was I alone in feeling this isolation? I don't think so. Although the boy and his baby sister didn't question their total belongingness, the grown-ups must have sensed, however fleetingly, their isolation. Grandfather, having realized that he muttered to the air, lapsed into silence. The students argued with no conviction that they could persuade. Men and women greeted one another and then joined their own gender circle. Living each in his or her own space, not really connecting, is universal rather than just a case of modern individuality and isolation. The stories that people tell—and people tell stories all over the world—support this somber picture. A common theme in them is the failure to reach mutual understanding on anything other than the most mundane matters. The failure is not with outsiders, which is understandable, but with people we know well–members of the family and community.

What, then, is the remedy? One remedy is to make personal stories bland and to project strong feelings onto the oversize personae of myths and sagas and, in our day, the heroes and villains of blockbuster movies.

OVERCOMING ISOLATION

Of the various ways to overcome isolation the most basic is bodily contact. In a hunting-gathering band, huddling, fondling, and caressing occur frequently not only between adults and children, but also among adults. Young men, in particular, sleep together in clusters, with arms and legs slung over one another's bodies as though they are lovers. Bodily contact establishes a feeling of oneness so strong that it can trump, in loyalty and allegiance, even close kinship ties.[5] Communal singing is another way to overcome isolation. In preliterate and folk communities, people find occasion to sing together, and in doing so they establish reassuring bubbles of sound around themselves. Everyone participates. The singing has no listeners—no outsiders to evaluate the performance and so make the singers feel self-conscious. Because looking tends to create distance, eyes may be shuttered in communal singing to enhance the sensation of total immersion. Individuals can blissfully lose their burdened selves in the larger whole.[6]

Working together creates communal feeling. In a poem called "Neighbors," David Allen Evans (b. 1940) has a couple cleaning the opposite sides of the same window pane. "He squirts Windex/ at her face;/ she squirts Windex/ at his face."[7] They seem to be waving to each other with their rag, but they are not: they are simply engaged in a common task. They are at one in that task, with a greater degree of closeness than if they wave rather self-consciously in greeting. Working together in the field, planting or harvesting, produces a sense of oneness that, at the same time, is also a oneness with nature. Even the bystander who happens upon the scene may find himself identifying with the farmers and the natural environment, inducing in him a feeling of calm.

Soldiers on the march, even more than farmers planting seedlings in a row, lose their individuality in the group. As for people watching on the sideline, they, too, lose their individuality, being irresistibly drawn into the marching column by the hypnotic power of synchronized motion, swelled further by the sound of martial music. The result of such merging for both soldiers and spectators is not calm but something equally—and perhaps even more—satisfying: namely, power.

SPEECH BINDS FOR GOOD AND ILL

People feel they live in the same world in large part because they apply the same words to the same things. If I am not a botanist, why do I still want to know the name of a flower? What additional information do I gain when I am told that I am looking at an African violet, a specimen of the *Saintpaulia ionantha*? None. Knowing its name reassures me not because I know more about a plant, but because I now share one more term—and, therefore, one more bit of the world—with my fellows. Although words held in common bind, to perform that function effectively there mustn't be too many of them. And there aren't. In fact, conversational vocabulary of the sort we use in daily life is surprisingly small: in modern society, it may not be many more than a hundred words. Important to social binding is not just a shared vocabulary, but also a distinctive way of pronouncing the words. Every close-knit group, linguists tell us, has it own quirks of speech that sets itself off from others.

If the group is sufficiently isolated, over time its speech becomes a language that no one outside the group can understand. The physical isolation is a sort of prison, and the language developed in it a further source of isolation–a further cutting off of stimulus from the outside world. The result is—what? Even under severe constraints people are ingenuous enough to make a liveable world; so liveable to them, in fact, that they do not recognize the constraints, have no idea that their sensory and mental capabilities are insufficiently challenged. What does the outside world make of this isolated people with their distinctive language and culture? To this question, I answer with a story—a true story.

Deep in the mountains of southwestern China near the border with Vietnam, two American scientists happen to meet in a government guest house. One—Gary Shook—is an entomologist; the other—Jamin Pelkey—is a linguist. Shook is collecting tiger beetles in Yunnan and is pleased to have found four new species. Pelkey is collecting people and their languages. He has better luck, for he has found dozens of new Phula languages. And just as Shook, the entomologist, would want to preserve as many species of tiger beetle as possible, so Pelkey, the linguist, would want to preserve as many of his newly found languages as possible. Beetles are, after all, the treasure trove of entomologists. In the same way, cultures and languages are the treasure trove of linguists. Moreover, exotic beetles and peoples have the potential to become future tourist attractions. What cultural preservationists overlook is that, whereas beetles are genetically programmed to know only one unchanging world—the world of beetles—the isolated peoples in southwestern China, now confined to the narrow reality of their culture and language, can with sufficient encouragement and the right opportunity break out and become entomologists, linguists, world citizens, just like Gary Shook and Jamin Pelkey![8]

THE ENVIRONMENT-PEOPLE BOND

Speech not only binds people, but also people with their environment, both bindings being necessary to human survival. Earlier, I drew attention to the importance of group singing in promoting "oneness." Words are sung, even though the feeling of "oneness" can be achieved with music alone. Why, then, use words? The answer is, unlike the sounds of music, words can explicitly link humans to elements of the nonhuman environment, and they do so most effectively as metaphors and similes. In the English-speaking world, we may say of a woman that she is a rose or a prickly pear, of a man that he is a fox or a pig, and we use such expressions—linking a human being with a plant or an animal—without thinking them at all strange. The same goes for the topographical features. We use anatomical metaphors, such as foothills and headlands or the spine of a ridge and the mouth of a river, in both common and technical speech, unbaffled by the usage, and, in the process, make objects unlike us in every way have the familiarity of our own body. Of course, different languages have different metaphors, but universal in all languages are words that identify humans with nonhuman elements. When such words are not only said but sung, our emotional bond with the environment significantly deepens.

Besides the natural environment, the built environment—city, town, neighborhood, or house—is also our home. The size of the home or habitat affects the closeness of the bond: the smaller the size, the more intimate, in large part because in a small space all our senses, and not just the visual, can be fully engaged. We respond, for example, to our hometown and to our home differently. Our hometown may occasionally present itself to us as a view—a composition of church, market square, and playground—but not the house or building we live in, which is not so much a view as a world of sensations and memories that, in the course of time, becomes as familiar as the clothes we wear. And just as we can grow attached to old, comfortable clothes, so we can grow attached to a house or residential building that has no architectural distinction. Attachment grows on us subconsciously. Children, especially, soak up its qualities and moods without knowing they are doing so. For this reason, our childhood home is imbued with a denser penumbra of meaning than the home or homes we have lived in as adult.[9] Even for us adults, home temporarily acquires this denser meaning when we are sick and in bed, cared for by others, sunk in puffy pillows and rumpled sheets, half-awake in a phantasmagorial world of subdued sounds, colors, and odors. And then there is the fact that we sleep at home. To the question, "What is the one special thing about home that distinguishes it from all other places?," we may be stumped for an answer, yet what can it be other than, "Every night we regularly lose our distancing consciousness, our identity and self, in restorative oblivion?"

Attachment to home has another source—stability. People have moods. Children learn early in life that they cannot always count on their parents' attention much less their smiles, a lesson in human unpredictability that has to be learned over and over again. Children themselves are noted for their changing moods, crying one moment and laughing the next. Adults, though relatively more stable, quarrel and make up and even fall in and out of love with surprising ease. Can one count on one's friends? Dr. Johnson says of friendship that "there is no human possession of which the duration is less certain."[10]

In the face of such human inconsistencies, home and its furnishings provide anchorage, an important service that can make us sentimental. I confess to it myself. When I leave my apartment on a longish journey, I pause at the door for a last look. I look back at the sofa with the slight hollow where I normally sit, the pile of unread magazines, the faux-Tiffany reading lamp, the cherry-wood kitchen table, the rows of books, CDs, and DVDs on the shelves and feel grateful that, when I return, they will be waiting for me exactly as they are now, with just a thin coating of dust to indicate that time has passed. This intimate bond leads to another thought: although I don't regard home as me, I can't help feeling that, with the cessation of breath, the "I" that lingers a little longer is not the corpse but rather my home, a unique arrangement of furniture, books, pictures, and knickknacks that is me, before it, too, is dismantled and dispersed.[11]

Bonding is not necessarily desirable. Marriages and families, far from being sweet unions, can be Alcatrazes of fear and hatred. Bonding with an environment, however, doesn't have quite such dire consequence. Dwellers in the rainforest occasionally wish to be free of the ceaseless rain and the ear-splitting screech of monkeys, but, on the whole, their forest is to them a haven and a source of sensorial delight. To outsiders who have strayed into it and lost their way, it can be a nightmare: the dense vegetation, the stifling heat, the clinging moisture, and the nauseous odor of decay all seem to hold them in malicious embrace, intent on reabsorbing them into nature's deep sleep. Mountains may be uplifting to mountain dwellers, but, to people habituated to open space and the big sky, they can induce claustrophobia, with every view blocked by a stony face. Even the tropical island—paradise not only to locals, but also to visitors— can, at times, seem a perfumed prison. As for the built environment, consider the house. Its character as haven can be overturned by a single event—a suicide or murder, for example. The house then seems to concentrate evil, trapping it in its nooks and corners, couches and curtains.

We speak of the haunted house. Horror movies are mostly set indoors and not in the great open spaces where cleansing winds blow. But, then, why does "haunted" suggest something bad? Why can't a house be haunted by benevolent spirits? It can, only we don't hear about it as often. My apartment, for instance, is in a 1906 landmark building that was at one time an elementary school. The words "Doty School" are still carved in the stone frieze over the front gate. When I am unable to sleep at night, I try to evoke the reassuring patter of little feet. The children who once ran through the building have given it an ineffable air of wholesomeness.

COMMUNAL BOND AND THE OTHER

People bond when they recognize their individual powerlessness in the face of an external challenge, which is, first and foremost, nature. Hunters have so bonded since the earliest times. The nature they depended on and contended with were wild animals. Chasing them required hunters to be frequently on the move. Their camps were temporary, which meant that the social relationships in them had to be fluid and simple, in contrast to those in farming communities. The nature that farmers have to contend with revolves around soil and weather. Group effort directed at nature and the bonding that results is evident in compact villages, work teams, communal feasts and communal worship, and people gathering informally to gossip and relax under the shade of a tree.

Besides nature, real or perceived human rivals and enemies are a reason for forming strong, communal bonds. In eighteenth-century England, young laborers channeled their energies into vicious sports—team against team, village against village. French farmhands were even more violent, perhaps because they, compared with their English counterparts, had more *fête* days. Workers from one village walked five or ten miles to another village just to start a brawl. Such uncalled for hostility against outsiders, to the extent it promoted internal cohesion and camaraderie, made social sense.[12]

Intense communal life was also an urban phenomenon in pre-modern times. Think of Shakespeare's Verona and the solidarity generated by contests between the Montagues and Capulets. Even the smallest, perceived slight could lead to bloodshed. Larger than the city and the city-state of Renaissance Europe is the nation-state of the early modern period. The nation-state is less homogeneously constituted than the city-state, being made up of diverse peoples who have little in common and hence little social contact in times of peace. Nevertheless, when an external enemy threatens, even the pluralistic nation-state can become for the duration a warmly cohesive whole—one large "family."

Life inside a community is sustained by an exchange of goods and services. Exchange is especially frequent in pre-modern communities, the frequency being a requirement of need, even of dire necessity. Need, however, affects the psychology of exchange, distorting it so that helping another and giving generously to another have not quite the virtue—the selflessness—that we regard such acts today. A village or tribal chief, for example, may dispense material largesse to the extent that he seems to be depleting his own wealth, but he feels he has to do it to maintain his status, and he expects ample compensations in deferential service. The word "gift" has a different meaning from today, if only because in archaic and primitive communities no one ever gave anything—whether goods, services, or honors—without proper recompense. Giving, in other words, is only the first part of a reciprocal action, the other part of which is the counter gift.[13]

I have put "reciprocity" in a somewhat dark light. I do so to balance the positive meaning given to community in social-welfare literature. The inescapable ambiguity in all human relationships is captured by the double meaning of certain key words. Thus, "bond," as in communal bond, is good but comes uncomfortably close to bondage. "With" means "together" but also "against," as in fighting with (that is, against) an enemy. "Clinch" may mean the clinch of love or the clinch of combat, and combat itself can be a means to clinch (deepen) communal ties. Hostility alienates and distances, and yet it is also a kind of relationship, one that is regulated by rules and stops short of destroying the adversary. "Hostile," moreover, shares a root with "hospitable," which rather suggests that the host who comes to us with open arms has mixed feelings, for which neither word—hostile or hospitable—is suitable. What is needed is a new word, a hybrid: "hospitility."[14]

The family is commonly regarded as a model of human warmth. In it one finds mutual help and care, dictated by kinship ties as well as by social convention. Maybe so; but, if so, it is true only of modern, well-provisioned families in which members, other than the very young, enjoy a considerable degree of independence. In an older world of stark needs and human ties that could not be broken, the family was all too often the seat of frustration and hostility that periodically found release in violence. Peter Laslett (1915–2001) noted that, in the pre-modern world, "the worse tyrants among human beings, the murderers and villains, were jealous husbands and resentful wives, possessive parents and deprived children....Men, women, and children had to live very close together for a very long time to generate the emotional power that could give rise to a tragedy of Sophocles, or Shakespeare, or Racine."[15]

PRIMITIVE VS. ETHNIC

Small, primitive communities (primitive in the sense of "early" or "original") declined rapidly in number during the twentieth century. In their place politically conscious *ethnic* communities emerged. The differences between them are striking. Primitives, though they lived in small, isolated settlements, nonetheless believed that they were located at the population center of the world and that their culture was the most advanced. They could so believe because they encountered few outsiders. The explorers and anthropologists who visited them did so separated by years, and they were often the same people. Moreover, they seemed most eager to find out how they—the locals—lived, their beliefs and values. Understandably, the locals concluded that the outsiders came in search of knowledge and wisdom. In sharp contrast, by the second half of the twentieth century, ethnics know they are only one group among many and that, moreover, they live at the margins of a far more powerful people and culture. In other words, primitives were able to muster a self-confidence, albeit one based on misunderstanding, that was not available to the ethnics.

Another important difference is this: the primitives—from simple hunter-gatherers and pastoral nomads to agriculturalists at various levels of material advancement and, indeed, wherever the sun and other heavenly bodies were clearly visible—lived not just on the land and its resources, but in a larger entity called the cosmos. The sun especially mattered to them as both a guide to the practicalities of life and as a distant, presiding deity that elevated them from the mundane and gave them not only comfort, but also a largeness of spirit. In this sense, the simplicity of their material culture notwithstanding, all of these peoples were cosmopolites.[16]

COSMIC CITY AND UNIVERSALISM

The city is from the start cosmopolitan, not a market town that has grown large through the gradual accretion of trade and people but rather heaven transposed to Earth or, alternately viewed, Earth raised to heaven. What planners seek is order and predictability that exist only in heaven—in the motion of the stars. The earliest cities appear to have started as ceremonial centers of cosmic scope—temples and ceremonial compounds of geometric shape (square or rectangle) oriented to the cardinal points.[17] To build such a center requires, minimally, knowledge of astronomy and how to organize humans into efficient labor teams. It requires the removal of villages, leveling of hills, filling of valleys, and diversion of streams. All the irregularities of Earth must make way for the geometry of heaven. Once built, people swarm in to service the palaces and the temples and their ruling elites. In time, as population continues to grow, the ceremonial character of the original construction is buried under the houses, shops, and streets of economic life. Activities and occupations multiply, turning the original ceremonial center into a profane world of merchants, shopkeepers, and craftsmen.[18]

The cosmic city does not exist in isolation. Other ceremonial centers also grow into bustling cities, linked to one another by highways that encourage the movement of people and trade. The political order that controls the wealthiest city and its region also exerts hegemony, if not quite total control, over other cities and regions, in which are located farms, villages, market towns, as well as enclaves of minority people. The political entity that embraces all is an empire.

An empire is cosmopolitan and universalist. It sees itself as "all under heaven" and, if not quite so boastfully, then as the center of the known world. *Tian xia* ("all under heaven") is how the Chinese see their empire. An empire—whether Chinese, Roman, or Inca—promotes uniformity. Its major cities have the same basic set of buildings, and these stand in a grid pattern—a rectangular arrangement of streets—that is symbolic of heavenly order. Beyond the symbolism the grid pattern also allows travelers to find their way and feel at home soon after they arrive at any city. Language, money, weights, and measures all tend toward uniformity. The people, too, are uniform and equal to the extent that they belong to the same social class or organization. Members of the same guild—such as carpentry, metal work, and the food industry—or profession—such as teaching, medicine, and law—dress and behave much alike. In the army, equality within the same rank is carried to the extreme such that individuals are, to all practical purposes, identical and exchangeable.

The forces for uniformity and equality suppress individual differences that, as noted earlier, are characteristic of the species. But, unlike the village or small town, contrary forces are also at work in the city, nation-state, and empire. Different hierarchies, each with its own ladder of success, give scope for individuals to develop their talents to the full and so differentiate themselves from their fellows. In other words, civilization encourages, on the one hand, uniformity/equality and, on the other hand, difference, ranked order, and individuality.

Commerce decisively encourages individuality because, as a way of life, it has never had a formal role in the cosmic city. Unlike farmers' activities of planting and harvesting, which have to adapt to the seasons and the passage of the sun, those of traders and merchants are far less dependent on solar events and the sort of cooperativeness that comes with the need to adapt. Farmers are place-centered and rooted in land, homestead, and tradition. Traders and merchants are much less so; to succeed in their various enterprises, they must be willing to loosen ties to place and move into space, wherever opportunities beckon, and there live and work, if only temporarily, among strangers. In the marketplace, strangers may speak variant tongues and have different customs, but all share the mentality and language of counting (numeracy); and with counting—with numbers that expand linearly—they acquire a sense of time that is linear or directional rather than exclusively cyclical.

In social life, the loss in intimate ties with kinfolk and neighbors is compensated by friendship with strangers that builds on business transactions.[19] Initially cool and calculating, a measure of affection inevitably takes over if the transactions result in mutual benefit. Something like a loop is established when the affection that follows beneficial exchange gives rise to and strengthens trust, and trust, in turn, is the foundation on which further trade negotiations and exchanges rest. Unlike the bonds of an agricultural community, friendship between merchants and traders is more a matter of choice—a relationship between individuals. To be an individual—a self—one has to maintain a certain distance from the other. Traders do not meet every day, their tasks not being communal, as are those of peasant farmers. A temporal disconnect, now and then, can actually strengthen a relationship in that each, having pursued his own course, will have more to offer the other when they meet. Where geographical distance is unavailable, the advantage of maintaining a certain distance translates into a need for privacy: a space of one's own in which to reflect, recuperate, plan, and luxuriate in just being one's self or possibly to reconcile the self's different moods and personas.[20]

CHAPTER 7
Segmentation and Self

———————————————————

T HE RISE OF THE INDIVIDUAL is a phenomenon of all complex societies. It reaches a peak, however, in the West, so I
now turn to Europe in the period from the Middle Ages
to the late nineteenth century. To make the task manageable, I propose to show
the rise of the individual and, with it, an increasing need for privacy in three
socio-cultural domains: the house and domestic space, food and table manners
(etiquette), and the world of theater.

THE HOUSE AND DOMESTIC SPACE

In medieval Europe, the manor house was essentially just one
large, undifferentiated room or hall. All sorts of activities occurred in it, just
as all sorts of activities occurred in the marketplace. The difference between
indoors and outdoors was minimal. When people stepped indoor in winter, they could feel somewhat sheltered from the elements, but the hall was
drafty and not really warm, despite the central fire. For this reason they did
not remove their cloak or their hat, and they continued to stand, for there were
few benches to sit on. Some stood around to talk business and politics; some
exercised their legs and danced; some ate or tried to sleep in a corner. A musician played his instrument, barely heeded, as children and dogs raced around,
the children shouting and the dogs barking. Indoors was as hectic as outdoors.
No privacy existed anywhere, and none was wanted.

The first real change was the addition of rooms at the two ends of the hall.
One eventually became a place for withdrawal, a bedroom; the other became
a kitchen. Over time domestic space was more and more segmented and spe-
cialized for the elites of Europe, culminating in the Victorian house, which
had—beside bedrooms and a kitchen—a drawing room, dining room, morning room, music room, nursery for children, boudoir for the ladies, smoking
room plus library for the gents, and, below stairs, the servants' quarters. And,
yes, there was also the vestigial hall, now reduced to just a narrow corridor at

which people still stood, as their ancestors did in the medieval hall, but only briefly to remove their overcoats and hats. The ideal of privacy peaked in the Victorian house. Children had their own quarters, supervised by a governess with her own quarters; master and mistress frequently slept in separate rooms. A woman in her boudoir could powder her face and regain her composure; a man in his library could smoke a cigar and blow rings into the air.

With the desire for privacy came the desire for interior life. A heightened sense of self gained ground over a period of some three centuries. By the mid-1500s, the communal bench gave way to the chair and then to the padded chair. The advantage of the padded chair is that one could sink into an enveloping space of one's own and stay there with comfort. The popularity of wall mirrors toward the end of the seventeenth century implied that people liked to look at and admire themselves in full length. By the eighteenth century, the library was a regular feature of gentry and aristocratic homes. A man could go there to let off his guard and relax and also to study, reflect, and enter worlds and times not his own. Books filled the shelves. Were they thought to be too intimate and revealing for the public eye? Whatever the reason, they were—for a time—hidden behind glazed panels or curtains. These devices to hide were removed when the master of the house recognized that books could advertise his good taste: thus, it would seem that the desire for social approval warred with the desire to develop the inner self.

FOOD AND ETIQUETTE

The story of food and etiquette shows certain parallels with the story of domestic space and its furnishings: both turn on partitioning (segmentation) and specialization. In medieval times, quantity mattered more than quality. The rich ate much, the poor little: that, rather than flavor, was the real distinction. Two kinds of foods went into the gullets of the rich, neither very appealing to modern taste. One was a mixed grill in which an extraordinary variety of none-too-fresh meats and vegetables (even flowers) were tossed in. The other was the whole animal—boar, pig, or deer. Culinary progress took the form of using fewer ingredients, a much greater appreciation of their distinctive flavors, separating the meats such that one followed another rather than thrown together, separating meats and vegetables, and not allowing the whole animal, or even a large recognizable chunk of it, from being brought to the dinner table.

Improved table manners might be taken as another indicator of increasing self-consciousness, of a heightened sense of one's dignity as measured by one's distance from the animal state. In the Middle Ages, even the high-born ate with their hands. By the sixteenth century, an elegant diner dipped into the communal plate with only three fingers. Forks came into use first in Italy, then in Germany and England. Queen Elizabeth I (1533–1603) provided forks at her table, a novelty that her critics considered an affectation. The number of table utensils steadily rose. After 1800, a well-laid table flaunted fruit knives and forks as well as fish knives and spoons, coated in silver in the belief that contact with steel would spoil the foods' taste. In the late seventeenth century, each guest was allowed one wine glass even though several wines were served. By the late 1800s, more than a half-dozen glasses might be used for the sherry, Bordeaux, Burgundy, Moselle, Tokay, Port, and Madeira. A glittering array of crystal and silverware greeted guests entering the dining room. Even before the first dishes were put on the table, it already groaned with utensils of high culture.

As noted earlier, medieval halls were very sparsely furnished. At dinner time tables were put up and benches and stools were brought in. The bench was the most common type of seat. People shared a bench at the dinner table as though they had no claim to being individuals. Only the great sat in chairs. They, alone, were individuals—people with authority, and "authority" meant the ability to be author or agent. I speak from experience, for, as an under-graduate at Oxford, my fellow students and I sat on benches when we dined in hall, and it was clear we were not considered fully formed human beings. At the high table the dons sat in chairs and commanded their own space, each a unique individual. I dreamed of occupying a chair at the high table one day and even of being a chaired professor, someone who has earned the right to speak ex cathedra.

"All the world is a stage," wrote William Shakespeare (baptized 1564–1616). And, by that, he meant that the stage represents the world; it is not only a model of the world, but holds a mirror to the world. Unlike literary or architectural achievements, the theater mirrors the world in two ways, one reinforcing the other: the play's story line and the physical arrangements of the theater. The history of theater is, in a nutshell, a movement from cosmos to landscape, from public square to drawing room, from participation to spec-tatorship, from communal rites that addressed sin and salvation, through the tragedy and farce of social intercourse to the inability to connect, the loneliness of the self, and private despair.

The modern play has roots in the rituals of the medieval church. The first major changes toward secular drama occurred during the twelfth cen-tury: moving the rituals outside the church building to unconsecrated public space; increasing the use of actors rather than clergy to perform in plays that still closely reflected Christian doctrine and ritual; separating the actors from spectators; and, if we think of the spectators as a congregation, then the move amounted to a progressive disengagement of people from the clergy and ordi-nary life from the sacred rites. A Corpus Christi drama, popular from 1300 to 1600, shows something of the spatio-temporal scope and the essentially reli-gious nature of the performances of that period. The space needed to enact the drama was no less than Heaven and Earth, and the time line was equally all-encompassing, for it began with the Fall and ended with the Last Judgment. Obviously, there could be no scenery for a play that embraced nearly the whole of space and time, and none was provided. Instead, there were isolated props, such as a bench for Noah's Ark, a painted canvas for the Red Sea, and a tree stump for the cross. Actors performed around one prop and then moved on to another.

Sacred plays gave way to morality plays, which, though they still drew on biblical themes, contained secular elements that took on, increasingly, humor and even ribaldry. Clergy stopped participating altogether. The actors were all quasi-professionals. By the time of Elizabeth I, plays showed everyday life and real people rather than allegorical figures. They became popular entertainments, yet the didacticism of the morality plays lingered. Moreover, the plots, though they no longer spanned from the Fall to the Last Judgment, still had global scope: Shakespeare's outdoor theater was the Globe (c. 1598) and appropriately so, for his dramas involved the mighty and the lowly, kingdom and market square, garden and wild nature—a universe, a world, not a landscape and certainly not the domestic space of private individuals. For this reason, Shakespearean dramas could only be enacted on a more or less bare stage. Scenery as such made an appearance during the 1700s, when the trend was away from high politics and war to private lives, a trend that culminated in misunderstandings within the family, which all took place in one room—the living room—by the second half of the nineteenth century.

As the play's themes moved toward the individual and private lives, the physical arrangements of space in the theater moved toward increasing separation and demarcation. In morality plays, actors and spectators freely intermingled, in part because performance space was not clearly demarcated from spectator space. Even when the two spaces were sharply drawn, as with the appearance of the proscenium arch, privileged spectators of the eighteenth century still felt no compunction sitting on the stage or moving onto it while the play was in progress. Only in the course of the nineteenth century, with the adoption of such successive steps as the introduction of the curtain, the darkening of the hall, and the increasingly private (domestic) nature of the dramas, was rigid separation between spectators and actors enforced.

The spectators themselves behaved more formally. In medieval times, they stood and milled about the play area, chattering among themselves and only periodically attending to the performance. In Shakespeare's time, some stood and some sat, and there was far greater interest in what the stage had to offer, if only because they paid for it. Those who sat sat on benches or chairs, depending of their status. Eventually, all spectators were granted the dignity of sitting in chairs, which, though closely packed, still allowed each person his or her space. Moreover, enveloped in the darkness that became the fashion during the late nineteenth century, they could believe themselves alone. Watching what? Not Heaven and Earth, Kingdom and Principality, but private house and private lives. In *A Doll's House* (1879), the play by Henrik Ibsen (1828–1906), Nora leaves her husband and children to discover who she really is. Peer, in Ibsen's play, *Peer Gynt* (1876), is driven to discover the self at whatever cost to others. Near his journey's end he peels an onion and finds to his horror that it has no heart—the self is untenanted at the core. In *The Seagull* (1896), the play by Anton Chekhov (1860–1904), Treplef asks plaintively, "Who am I? What am I?"

By the 1900s, the West had come to think that individualism had gone too far, that people felt isolated and anxious, that all the material gains did not compensate for the lack of passionate engagement with one another. In pondering how people's lives can be made more meaningful, words such as "community" and "neighborhood," which evoke a pre-modern stage of belonging and cooperation, found favor among social reformers and planners. These and other warm-puppy words today are contrasted with society, civilization, and individualism, all of which suggest isolation, coolness, and impersonality.

Would spatial re-integration be the answer? Planners and architects seem to think so, for an architectural trend since the second half of the twentieth century is to re-integrate space, joining living room with dining room and minimally separating the kitchen from the dining area in the house; and, in the theater, it has become fashionable to remove the proscenium and curtain and let the stage protrude into the space occupied by the audience so that it and actors can feel that they live in a common world. Social reformers feed the nostalgia by romanticizing the pre-modern community.

In time, the word "individualism" has come to mean not the realization of an individual's potential—including the potential to be wise and good—but mere selfishness. A historical process that, over the centuries, has allowed human beings to become more fully themselves is thus seen in a negative light. The modern cosmopolitan city, in particular, is all too commonly regarded as the place where the ego is allowed full play to the detriment of communal bond.[3]

The City as a Moral Universe

WHAT IS THE TRUER PICTURE? The news media make us face the dark side of urban sprawl—anomie, despair, violence, and absence of neighborliness-all of which seem confirmed as we walk about any city and see with our own eyes dilapidated and abandoned houses, pot-holed streets and graffiti-covered walls. Most American cities have a bright side, however, made up of places that cast about them pools of well-being, such as a children's museum, library, bandstand for Sunday afternoon concerts, theme park, shopping arcade, public swimming pool that turns into a winter skating rink, games arcade for teenagers, and recreation center for seniors. When an improvement first appears in the city, we may take notice and give thanks; but, unlike the peeling walls and pot-holed streets, which seem permanent eyesores and never cease to irritate, the innovations and improvements—even major ones—are quickly taken for granted. Wheelchair ramps in public spaces are an example. These shovel-shaped indentations on the sidewalk curbs, accentuated in some cities by painted yellow borders, were built at great public expense. They are an emblem of civilization, yet who now see them with a sense of civic pride?

A common accusation against the city and even the suburb is that the concept of neighborliness seems lost. Even the people who live next door can be strangers. When one runs out of sugar or is in need of help with the storm windows, one can't just knock on the door of the adjacent apartment or house. On the other hand, in the city and suburb it can happen that everyone in urgent need of help is treated as a fellow human being—a neighbor. The following three stories illustrate my point.

I begin with an incident that happened to me several years ago. I was in London's Underground, changing trains to go to a friend's place and stay with him overnight before catching a plane back to my home in America. I carried two suitcases up a steeply sloping escalator. A man accidentally gave me a push as he passed by. I fell backward and knocked my head against the sharp edge of a rising step. The escalator was promptly stopped. Blood oozed out from the back of my head. An Underground official rushed up with a first-aid kit. He put his arm around my shoulder and said that an ambulance had been called and would be here soon. In what seemed to be no time at all, medical assistants arrived to help me into a waiting vehicle, which started its sirens and raced through London's streets to the emergency room of a city hospital. There, doctors and nurses danced to my attendance. In the midst of all this activity, and even though I was in a daze, I wondered that the city should put so many of its resources at my disposal. For who was I? A non-tax-paying stranger from the other side of the Atlantic; yet, for a spell, Londoners treated me as they would a neighbor.[1]

And now, two other stories. Both are set in the United States. The first draws on the biography of a young man, José, who as an eight-year-old child fell seriously ill. High fever gave him periodic seizures. He soon assumed the posture and behavioral traits of a brain-damaged, autistic youth. The threat of seizures kept him at home for the next fifteen years. His condition steadily deteriorated until he was sent to a state hospital. That move, which might be expected to lead to his complete incapacitation, proved to be his first step toward recovery.

At its worst, a state hospital for the mentally disturbed is a "total institution" geared to the degradation of its patients. The neurologist Oliver Sacks (b. 1933) admitted as much in his report on José. On the other hand, when the hospital functions as it should, it is a refuge for tormented and storm-tossed souls. A state hospital happened to provide José with exactly what was needed—a mixture of order and freedom from the confusion and chaos that resulted, in part, from epilepsy and, in part, from the turmoil of his home life. Home made demands, even as it protected and gave shelter: the constant care and worry of family members were in themselves a tyrannical demand. After the moral closeness and febrile intimacy of his house, José suddenly found himself in a professional world of strangers who were "unjudging, unmoralistic, unaccusing, detached," but who, at the same time, could show "a real feeling both for him and his problems." The hospital, like a great metropolis, does not judge or accuse; it is coolly amoral.[2]

The second example is a work of fiction—a short story by John Updike (1932–2009) called "The City." I use it rather than a sociological account, because of its exceptional observational detail—material, social, and psychological—that only a writer of Updike's caliber can gather and convey. And what is conveyed are not just the facts, telling as they are, but a whole urban ethos and mood.

The story's chief protagonist is Carson, a former schoolteacher who, after a divorce and the breakup of his family, is a salesman for an equipment firm. He becomes seriously ill on one of the business trips. He checks into a downtown hotel and considers calling his family, only to remember that his ex-wife is remarried, and his daughter has disowned him and joined a feminist commune.

With the hotel doorman's help, Carson gets into a cab and eventually into the emergency room of a city hospital. There, predictably, he encounters a nightmare of bureaucratic obtuseness. Yet in time he is cared for, with a certain offhand efficiency. A number of checks must be followed through. An x-ray technician directs Carson to take a deep breath and hold it and then encourages him with a big-brotherly "good boy." In the next few hours, Carson is visited by several young nurses and interns. Finally, a little after midnight, a doctor arrives in a tweed jacket and tie. Carson wonders what dinner party he had just left. The hospital is a sick man's habitat, but he can see that the doctor is healthy and must have a home, family, and routine to return to. So how long would he want to stay? "I'd like to operate," the doctor says softly. He then stands up and takes off his coat, "as if to join Carson in some sudden, cheerfully concocted athletic event."

The days of recovery have their moments of simple happiness. For Carson there is a renewed, childlike appreciation of technology: the taut white bed with a handle that can lift and bend the mattress in several ways or a television set mounted high on the wall that obeys the light touch of a remote control. One night Carson falls asleep while the television is still on. A touch on his upper right arm wakes him. "He opened his eyes and there, in the quadrant of space where the rectangle of television had been, a queenly black face smiled down upon him, a nurse taking his blood pressure."

When Carson recovers sufficiently to move around, he observes his fellow patients. They are a motley group, reflecting the composition of the city and its surrounds. There are farmers with "crosshatched necks and hands that had the lumpy rounded look of used tools," "old ladies shriveling to nothing in a forest of flowers," "an immensely plump mocha-colored woman wearing a scarlet Hindu dot in the center of her forehead," and "a lean man whose shaved head had been split by a gash now held together by stitches." When Carson nods to him in hesitant greeting, he replied loudly, "Hey man," as if they share a surprising secret.

A few days later, a cab takes Carson to the airport. He sees little of the city on the way. "For an instant from the air a kind of map spreads itself underneath him, and was gone." Afterward, thinking back on "the farm voices, the far-off skyscrapers, the night visits of the nurses, the doctors in their unseen, unsullied homes," it seems Carson had "come to know the city intimately." Its citizens have bestowed themselves on him without his knowing their names.

The city is at the other end in scale from the family, to which I gave attention earlier. Contrary to popular depictions of these two social entities and in order to introduce a better balance in perceived value between them, I chose to emphasize disconnectedness within the family and connectedness within the city. The larger thesis is that, for humans, no matter what the warmth and duration of human contact and what the size of the group, a periodic sense of isolation is inescapable; it is no less than the human condition.

PART III

Frailties and Evils

The Seven Deadly Sins

T HE HUMANITIES HAVE HISTORICALLY been inclined to highlight achievements in the arts, literature, architecture, and, more recently, science. By temperament and upbringing, I share this sunny outlook and am therefore out of step with sophisticated opinion since 1900, which tends to dwell on human failings and shrug off the good qualities as sentimental or naive. To Walter Benjamin (1892–1940), for example, the notion of "progress" is simply the last refuge of the intellectually philistine and the politically corrupt.[1] Dwelling on failings and evil can go too far, however, and take one perilously close to indulgence in masochism. Ignoring human failings obviously won't do either, if only because it runs smack against common experience.

What I propose to do, then, is to precede the bright side of the human story with the dark side, and in presenting the dark side I find that I follow, after all, a strain in the humanities that is not by any means commendatory. I refer to theology's reminders of our sinfulness, history's reminders of our capacity for evil, law's reminders of our dubiety and mischievousness, and classical literature's reminders of the immutable operations of fate.

I begin the dark side with certain innate defects of human nature, using the traditional "seven deadly sins" for convenience. Singly and in combination these sins impoverish life and make dreams of an ideal world or even just a decent human society seem utopian. Take, first, pride—Lucifer's sin and considered by Christianity to be the most deadly. Pride makes Lucifer see himself as God's rival, the source of value and creativity. But, then, Lucifer is an archangel! Few humans—perhaps only the mad—rise to that level of presumption. On the other hand, Western civilization does boast individuals whose exorbitant claims for humankind can seem a challenge to God. These individuals are not, however, just examples of modern hubris. In classical antiquity, Protagoras (c. 490–420 BCE) had already coined the phrase "man is the measure." But measure of what? Of everything? Whatever Protagoras had in mind, ancient Greeks generally refrained from extending the rule—"man the measure"—

beyond Earth and the human world to the cosmos. Placed against the cosmos they recognized their own insignificance. For this reason, they could find inspiration in a night sky filled with stars.

This frame of mind, one of humility vis-à-vis the cosmos, remained during subsequent expansions of human knowledge and power—notably, the Renaissance, the age of great explorations and great scientific discoveries. Only during the late twentieth century did a radical shift occur. In the academies, a style of thinking so expanded the imperium of human language that all, including the forces of nature and the cosmos itself, came under it. There is nothing outside verbal constructs, themselves subservient to social forces, to command respect and awe. The pride of such thinkers has become truly Luciferian. They have about them a jaded air, it being difficult to drum up enthusiasm when there is no knowledge, only knowingness, no progress in truth, only gain in sophistication, The good news is that the fad cannot be sustained. It already seems to be waning.

Covetousness, the next sin on the list, is less deadly than pride because it implied a lack and not a vaunting of self-sufficiency. One covets other people's possessions in the belief that having them will enhance one's own life. The desire, unworthy in itself, has the further disadvantage of being an illusion. Possessions do not have the power to enhance life in any real, tangible sense unless one has the knowledge, the time, and a proper state of mind to enjoy them. Otherwise, they clutter space and collect dust, their satisfaction reduced to the tawdry prestige of mere ownership.

Lust. Although its old meaning of pleasure and even playfulness is innocent enough, the meaning it has now is uncontrollable passion and naked power play. A lustful man is one who puts his own sensual intoxication ahead of any concern for the other. This is not only morally wrong, but it is also a feeble surrogate for true, erotic passion in which one self merges with the other, and for a while egoism disappears. Such a state is heavenly while it lasts, but it cannot, as the tragic romances of Tristan and Isolde of the twelfth century and of Romeo and Juliet (1597) remind us. In the imagination, erotic passion at its most intense culminates in Richard Wagner's (1813–1883) soaring aria, *Liebestod* ("Love Death" in German), from his opera, *Tristan und Isolde* (1865). What a contrast with Giacomo Castanova's (1725–1798) serial couplings and conquests that turn increasingly monotonous and boring as they drag on. In the end, they are only good for boasting.

The next two sins are anger and gluttony, different emotions and states of being, of course, but they have this in common: both are turbulent, barely controllable feelings in the self and, at the same time, targeted at something outside. Their difference lies in that, whereas anger seeks release by exiting from the self and destroying the other, gluttony futilely seeks relief by incorporating the other—food—into the self. In Western countries, both sins have declined sharply in modern times. One cause is a higher standard of living; another is a change in perception. Throughout the ages anger stood for masculinity and power. From the eighteenth century onward, however, it was to seem not strength but weakness, not a man in control but a child in tantrums.[3] As for gluttony, fewer famines made it less exigent; improved table manners made it less acceptable.

Envy, like covetousness, is pathetic and not a feeling that I, for one, would care to admit, for, whereas I may brag about my pride and anger, deeming the one proper self-esteem and the other an outburst of righteousness, I can hardly admit to being envious or covetous without drawing attention to a deficiency in me. And what is it that others have and I don't? Wealth? Power? Status? Reputation? Family happiness? Any one of them can boost my sense of self-worth, but to yearn for it is not only to admit a lack, but to make all too evident the absence of any core value in the depth of my being that leaves me vulnerable to other people's judgment and whim. Moreover, unlike the other sins, envy is especially deadly in that recognizing it is not necessarily liberating. On the contrary, dwelling on the feeling can be addictive, making one see what others have as simultaneously desirable in their exaggerated glamor and hateful in their unavailability.

Sloth, the last of the seven sins, is both a moral and an intellectual failing. It shows ingratitude for existence; it wastes the gifts of senses and mind that, properly used, reveal to us "the many splendored" works of creation; and it denies our nature as active beings, capable of evil but also of good.

CHAPTER 10

Other Evils

T HE SEVEN DEADLY SINS do not cover violence, cruelty, humiliating the other, and greed—sins that are much more in the minds of us moderns. Violence was simply taken for granted in an earlier age; likewise, cruelty–a word that is related to "crude." Violence, cruelty, and crudity go together, and all three subside as society becomes more affluent and civil. They are still with us, of course, but are artfully covered up. Humiliating the other is endemic to hierarchical societies and so is greed. I will now take up these non-canonical "sins."

THE VIOLENCE OF EATING

Violence is frowned upon by our, relatively speaking, tender-hearted age. When we refrain from not only physical, but even verbal violence, we may well think of ourselves as mild and peace-loving, forgetting, however, a violence we daily commit—eating. I remember watching a movie called *Mondo Carne* (1962) some years ago. The opening scene is a close-up of a mouth that shows two formidable rows of teeth lifting and lowering, as though chewing meat. There is something grossly animal-like about that mouth until the camera slowly retreats and reveals the entire face. It is that of Bertrand Russell (1872–1970) giving a philosophy lecture! Now that makes me feel better, though not for long. Sooner or later, I have to confront the fact that "eating and being eaten" rules the animal and human worlds.

Animals accept the violence of eating naturally. We humans can't quite manage, at least in those moments when we think about how our body is maintained. Some people—gatherers in tropical forests, for example—are lucky in that their diet consists largely of plant foods. In striking contrast, Inuits of the Arctic coast traditionally depend almost wholly on animals not only for food, but also for clothing and shelter. Blood and torn flesh are a regular and welcomed feature of their life. One way they ease their conscience is to show respect. A dead seal should not be laid on a dirty floor, and, while caribou hunting proceeds, the scraping, stretching, and sewing of skins to make clothes are strictly forbidden, for such activities are believed to wound the animal's soul. The idea that the hunted animal agrees to be caught and slaughtered is common among hunting tribes. It is a convenient belief, one that assuages guilt, but it is also rooted in a notion of reciprocity that governs all living things, the notion being, "Eat by all means if you also accept being eaten."[1]

Civilization covers up the animality of eating in a number of ways. One is to make it into a ceremony and an art form. Eating ceremonially asserts that one is human, not animal, civilized, not barbarian. As for food preparation, the Chinese are unique in that, since ancient times, they made a practice of shredding and mixing vegetables and meats to produce foods of differing texture, aroma, and flavor. Except for small crustaceans and fish, whole animals seldom appear on the table. Disseverment hides nature. Recombining the severed pieces makes cooking an art and the cook an artist with clean hands.

Eating etiquette and haute cuisine developed in the West, as I have noted. Only from 1700 onward did eating—first among the aristocracy and then among the bourgeoisie—become more and more a polished social occasion. People in their finery gather around a table glittering with glass and silverware and pretend they are more interested in conversation than putting food into their mouth. The food itself is less and less recognizable as animal corpses, being chopped up or covered in garnishments. Europe's high society resolutely turns its back on food's animal origin. In English-speaking countries, the practice of slicing a whole turkey at the dinner table is a relic of the past. Guests at the table are so desensitized that they hardly raise an eyebrow when the host passes around a large platter heaped with steaming flesh and asks, "Breast or leg?"

Attending to the gustatory pleasure of the moment, forgetting its source in a once-living creature, is necessary to our enjoyment of meat. Even more necessary—indeed, essential—is erasure from memory the total number of chickens, pigs, and cows that one has eaten in a lifetime. Hundreds? Who is perverse enough to estimate? This is the sort of fact we do rather not know. We don't want to know, for example, that, in one year, Americans will consume some 35,000,000 cows, 115,000,000 pigs, and 9,000,000,000 birds.[2]

CRUELTY TO ANIMALS, DESECRATION OF NATURE

Hunters can be cruel to animals, but it is in agricultural societies that cruelty reaches the pits. The abattoirs of the world are hellholes of pain. Animals are not only slaughtered for food and raw material, but also "broken" in and trained to do human society's heavy work. The procedures that convert a spirited animal into a tame one vary in brutality. Among the worst is castration. Here is a lurid account from Cuba: "The bull's testicles were tied with a thick wire and then stretched out onto an iron and stone anvil. With a sledgehammer the testicles would be pounded until the tendons and connections to the rest of the body were severed. Only the bags remained hanging and in time would wither away. The pain suffered by these bulls was so intense that one could tell when the testicles had been destroyed because the animal's teeth would loosen. Many died, but others survived and were no longer bulls but oxen, that is, tame castrated beasts used to pull the plow."[3]

Some animals are turned into pets. From a psychological viewpoint, human consciousness of power reaches a peak when one can play with a living creature and do whatever one likes with it, rather than for an economic purpose that narrows one's range of choice. The molding starts with breeding, which may be continued over successive generations, to produce an animal of a shape and size, and temperament that tickle the human whim.

The oldest animal domesticate—the dog—is so altered that its size varies from a Chihuahua to a St. Bernard, a forty-time difference in weight. It is hard to believe that they belong to the same species, and, indeed, interbreeding is impossible for obvious physical reasons. Although dogs were bred for practical use—even the poodle was originally a hunter—they eventually became pets, a bundle of hair to put on one's lap, as with a Pekinese, or made to "sit," "beg," "fetch," or "roll over" on command, as with many other breeds. What is it in our perverse psychology that gives us satisfaction when we extract instant obedience? The larger the beast, the more its submissiveness and humiliation feed our ego. At the zoo among the most popular shows is to see the elephant, an animal of great natural dignity, wearing a tutu that barely covers its ample waist, rearing up and balancing awkwardly on top of a ball.

Dogs and elephants offer their human masters the power of humiliating obedience. Goldfish offer their owners something else—the pleasure of turning living creatures into works of art. Shape and color of the fish rather than their behavior are the challenge to human ingenuity. The species is naturally polymorphous. Chinese fanciers, noting this trait, have sought since the Song Dynasty (960–1279) to increase it. And so to the original greenish and grayish colors were added gold, red, and such multi-hues as gold and white, red and black and white, vermilion and white, with the colors appearing in patches, spots, or bands. Fanciers also sought to increase the number and size of fins, a desideratum of which is that they wave like veils in a summer breeze. Aesthetics all too easily degenerates into cruelty as when the eyes are bred to become hugely bulbous and protuberant, making them vulnerable to attack by other fish or to damage when they bump against a rock or wall.

Many animals have thus been bred for human use and pleasure. So far, humans themselves have been exempt, with the single exception of the slave farm, in which slaves, selected for their size and strength, were encouraged to reproduce for their master's profit. Disciplining humans so they are little more than beasts of burden or performing animals is something else, a temptation that makes it unnecessary for them to try the longer and more tedious route of breeding. But the temptation is there, and, given modern techniques of genetic engineering, the possibility exists that, one day, the powerful-and-mad might treat humans as genetic plasticine to be altered upon a whim. Already we have a hint of what can happen in the dwarfs and midgets that Renaissance potentates kept in their households as pets or as curiosities that could be passed around to satiate a peculiar taste.[4]

I have dwelled on man's treatment of animals as shorthand and emblem of man's treatment of nature generally. That treatment has been consistently harsh ever since agriculture was invented. Why care about streams and lakes, trees and grass, when animals with whom we are closer kin do not receive such care? By "care" I don't just mean seeing to it that soil is not over-used and streams over-fished, for such activities clearly harm our own livelihood and well-being; rather, I have in mind a larger view and a more generous spirit in which we see nature as a wonder in its own right, quite apart from its usefulness to us, and see ourselves as a part of nature, both dependent on it and able to contribute to it. To be sure, humans have conceived less anthropocentric views from time to time. Taoism, Hinduism, Buddhism, and Franciscan adoration of nature and the modern ecological movement are examples, but their ability to conserve nature is minimal, with the modern ecological movement a possible exception. How many trees has Taoism saved in China? Small clusters around the Taoist temples were all the religion could save, even though millions of Chinese were Taoists at one time.

Given the disjunction between belief and action in regard to nature, it is hardly surprising that the same disjunction holds in regard to people. Even in Buddhist and Christian countries, for all the preaching and writing only a small proportion of needy people have benefited from genuine compassion and love. As for the rest, the relationship between the powerful and the powerless is typically one of domination and exploitation. What makes this lopsided relationship possible and even natural to the powerful is that they regard the people under them as subhuman—animals. Jean-Paul Sartre put it thusly: "In the eyes of the rajahs, the pearlfisher did not differ much from the pig that noses out truffles; the labor of the lacemaker never made of lace a human product; on the contrary, lace made a laceworm of the lacemaker."[5]

DOMINATION IN HIERARCHICAL SOCIETIES

All complex societies are hierarchical, though the rigidity of the hierarchy and the social differences between the ranks vary. Two civilizations—Chinese and Indian—lie at opposite extremes. China has traditionally recognized four classes: scholar-official, farmer, artisan, and merchant. To the Chinese way of thinking, farmers matter because they are engaged in "root" activities: they produce. Merchants, by contrast, are engaged in "branch" activities: they merely exchange what others produce. The Chinese cosmos, elaborated over time into a grand and intricate edifice, is geared to agriculture and has no place for commerce. Merchants may be rich, but their social status is low, unless they take on the trappings of the scholar-official class. As for farmers, those with access to education can, through passing a succession of examinations, become scholar-officials. Needless to say, opportunity for such upward mobility is limited, and only a tiny portion of peasant farmers can hope to rise above the status into which they were born. Moreover, although farmers command respect to a degree unparalleled in other stratified societies, a note of contempt lingers. For example, in the *Lu-shih Ch'un-ch'iu* (a third-century BCE compendium), farmers are praised because, in their primitive simplicity, they are quick to accept commands.[6]

India's social stratification, grounded in religious belief and practice, is rigid. The four traditionally recognized castes—the priestly and learned, warrior and ruler, farmer and merchant, and peasant and laborer—allow little mobility, though it can occur. There may not be much motivation for mobility, however. Warriors, like warriors everywhere, tend to show contempt for men of peace, the priests and the learned, even if they belong to a higher caste. As for those below the warrior caste, they are able to retain their self-esteem by seeing the priests and the learned (Brahmins) as parasites on society. Moreover, for all the inequality in the social system as a whole, within the same caste members have more or less equal status, on the basis of which they enjoy fellowship and share power; they may also feel superior to outsiders for religious reasons, even if the outsiders are materially better off.

The sharpest distinction in the Indian social system is between those who belong to a caste and those who lie outside it—the untouchables. The untouchables, who have the dirtiest jobs, are regarded as unclean; they pollute everything they touch, and, indeed, their very presence is considered polluting. On a cosmic scale of being, the outcast sweeper and manure carrier are outranked by the cow, peacock, monkey, and horse. This may seem outrageous to modern sensibility, yet in eighteenth-century England a similar attitude was indicated: one had only to compare the spacious, well-maintained horse stables on a nobleman's estate with the cramped cottages in which farm laborers lived. A nobleman clearly valued his pure-bred horses more, only this could not be openly acknowledged in a supposedly Christian country. Was this higher ranking of certain animals also true of China? I dare not believe that the Chinese were any different. Nevertheless, when a stable burnt down, Confucius (551–479 BCE) asked, "Are the men safe?" He did not inquire about the horses.

All "civilized" societies have adopted some form of slavery. That all over the world, and for so long, humans could be owned as property shows how little the powerful regarded the weak. The slaves' social standing varied notably, however, from society to society. Romans owned Greek slaves, who looked no different and who could well be better educated. For these and other reasons, they were treated reasonably well. In the Ottoman empire, well-educated white slaves could rise to the highest office. The dark-skinned suffered most, not necessarily in the physical sense, for white indentured servants could suffer as badly, but in humiliation. In the antebellum American South, Africans could be treated, at one extreme, as pets and sexual playthings and, at the other extreme, as draft animals and beasts of burden. Significantly, slaves preferred hard toil in the field to the indignity of pethood and sexual abuse in the big house.

In authoritarian societies, people other than members of the ruling class tend to be seen and treated as much alike. Democratic societies, in contrast, encourage the idea that people are individuals and different. Both types of society, however, have one institution in common—the military—and in it uniformity and obedience are the guiding principles. Consider boot camp training in America. Draftees come to the camp as individuals. The sergeant's job is to erase the individuality: everyone wears the same uniform, sports the same haircut, adopts a certain way of speaking, standing, sitting, eating, and making up their beds. Standardization makes soldiers so much alike that they can be as easily replaced as other types of military hardware. Moreover, depriving soldiers of the dignity of selfhood makes them more likely to obey unthinkingly. A periodic dose of humiliation helps. At a marine camp in South Carolina, when a staff sergeant says, "'Pick your nose,' fifty-seven index fingers shoot into the nostrils."[8]

HUMBLING ONESELF BEFORE POWER

A social class is made up of members of more or less equal standing. Social class is, however, a broad and abstract category, within which are institutions, such as the family, school, government bureau, or local business, where inequality blatantly remains. Consider traditional Chinese society. In the scholar-official class, a father's power in the family is absolute; he is sovereign over its members. A town's magistrate is, in turn, a father figure to his people and commands the highest respect. Kowtowing and slapping one's own face in acknowledgment of a fault are well-known ways of showing respect and humbling oneself.

How far can soul-blighting deference go? A story that dates back to the Tang Dynasty (618–907) is revealing. The younger brother of an official prepares to leave for his first posting. He promises his older brother that he will be patiently obedient in all his dealings with his superiors. "If they spit on me, I shall simply wipe my face without a word." "Oh, no!" replies the brother aghast. "They might take your gesture for an impudence. Let the spittle dry by itself."[9]

The prestige of power and the deference it commands are not by any means confined to despotic or authoritarian societies. Even citizens of the United States do not rise above the pathos. When John F. Kennedy, Jr. (1960–1999), died in an airplane crash, people lined up outside his New York City residence to pay homage. A twenty-nine-year-old salesman, Anthony Owens, was among them and in tears. Several years ago, Owens made a delivery to Kennedy's office building and spied him in the corridor. "I froze," he said. "Then I started shaking like this." He extended a trembling hand. "Mr. Kennedy asked me why I was so nervous and I said, 'You're a part of American history.' He told me that he was just like anybody else and offered me an autograph if I held the elevator."[10]

How does one rise to power in a stratified society? By merit, one likes to think, and it surely does happen; otherwise, it is hard to imagine such a society can sustain itself or even come into existence.

What about those who lack talent and drive? They can rise by flattery, which is not easy, for one has to know how to flatter and whom to flatter. Without family connections to the boss, one may have to begin by buttering up his underlings. Epictetus (55–135), the Greek Stoic philosopher who was born a slave, asked, "How many things must I endure to become a distinguished person—walk in splendor as a praetor and consul? Why, I might have to kiss the hands of other people' slaves."[11] This example, taken from the Roman Empire of the first and second centuries CE, may be a bit extreme, but something like it is nonetheless all too familiar even in a democratic society. Have I not brought flowers to the secretary and necktie to the male executive assistant so that their favor may smooth my path into the boss's inner sanctum?

GREED

Greed is an egregious temptation of civilizations. Those who have want more. It can be an addiction beyond control. Take the house or houses where the rich live. Is there an upper limit to their size, luxury, and number? Yes, surely, but the upper limit is set maniacally high. The rich and powerful in advanced civilizations appear to have no notion of the human scale—of restrictions dictated by the mere fact of possessing a body. In eighteenth-century England, for example, a duke might have ten seats, an earl nine, and a baron eight. These residences boasted many amenities and art treasures that enhanced the owner's status, if not necessarily his quality of life. Given almost unlimited wealth and means, whimsy inevitably came into play. One English castle, for example, was equipped with twenty pianos that apparently no one played. A duke owned 365 pairs of shoes, and an earl's castle had 365 rooms.[12]

So that we do not dismiss these numbers as mere historical curiosities, remember how many pairs of shoes Mrs. Imelda Marcus (b. 1929), the wife of a former president of the Philippines, had? A thousand? I was unbelieving and indignant when I read about her shoes, until I remembered that I, at my acquisitive peak, owned some 10,000 books, of which I couldn't have read more than a thousand from cover to cover. Why couldn't I control the itch to buy? Was it a feeling of emptiness that needed filling? Was it a desire to be admired for my catholic learning that a book-lined study might convey? And won't that desire itself be evidence of an underdeveloped, needy self?

KILLING AND WAR

The ease with which we kill begins with the matter-of-fact killing of animals. For hundreds of thousands of years, humans were hunters: the smell of blood filled our nostrils in every great hunt, and over time it couldn't help staining our being to the core. Killing extends from animals to humans, an easy step to take, for people habitually see others, not wholly unlike themselves, as not fully human.

Evidence for this perception is abundant. Most telling, because it is universal and because it can seem just a minor defect, is the way people have an honorific word for themselves that they do not extend to others. Take the five peoples who live in the northwestern quarter of New Mexico: Navaho, Zuñi, Mormon, Spanish-American, and Texan. The Navaho call themselves *dineh*—the people—with the implication that others do not quite measure up; the Zuñi's self-designation is *ashiwi*—"the cooked ones"—as distinct from those who are uncultured—"raw"; the Mormons see themselves as the Chosen People; the Spanish-Americans as *la gente*—"people," in the honorific sense; and the Texans are in their own eyes the only "real" Americans. True, these groups live in peace; they have to, being a part of the modern State of New Mexico. Denigrating the other, however, always runs the risk of inflammation into violence.[13]

The worst evil that humans commit against one another is war—at least in the scale of suffering and killing. War is so common that it is hard to imagine any history written without it. Take the ancient Greeks, a people we admire so much as progenitors of Western civilization. War was, to them, a fact of life. The city-states were almost constantly in armed conflict. The historian Thucydides (c. 460–c. 395 BCE) couldn't conceive of history as anything other than war, interrupted by peace. But let me turn to a less familiar example at the other end of the Eurasian continent—a period in China's past that historians rightly call the Warring States (403–221 BCE). The seven states were either at war or in anticipation of one, until they were unified by the Qin King in 221 BCE. He came to be known as the First Emperor. The seven states had much in common culturally. Unlike the Greek city-states, they were also much alike in political organization, the religious core of which was a cosmic worldview that, in ritual practice, required much shedding of blood. Violence was in the air. Hunting and war were the favorite and prestigious occupations of the upper class. The two occupations dovetailed into each other, their manner of attack being much the same, and so was the end result—fields of corpses.

René Grousset (1885–1950), a French sinologist, summarized the death toll as follows: "In 331 Ch'in captured the army of Wei and decapitated 80,000 men; in 318 they broke up the coalition of Wei, Han, and Chao, and cut off 82,000 heads; in 312 they beat Ch'u and 80,000 heads fell. In 307 they contented themselves with the score of 60,000 heads, but with the accession of King Chao Hsiang the scale of the massacres increased. In 293 he defeated Han and Wei and won himself, for a start, a trophy of 240,000 heads. In the campaign of 275 against Wei only 40,000 heads fell, but in a new expedition against the same adversary, a further 150,000. In 260 in a major success against Chao, although he had promised to spare the lives of the conquered, more than 400,000 were decapitated."[14]

These figures sound surreal, and one might consider them as suggestive only. But even as orders of magnitude they shock, especially because the massacre occurred not only during the heat of war, but also long afterward, when butchering the captured could be done methodically. How was the total deadening of moral sense possible? And how is it still possible, as the genocides and killing fields of our time attest?

Any answer must consider the following facts. First is our lust for meat, a food that can only be obtained by killing and dismembering creatures who are clearly our "semblables" and even our pals in another mood. The bloodstain on the kitchen counter doesn't bother us; and, as for the rivers of blood in the slaughterhouse, it is bad taste to mention them, and, of course, cookery books never do. Second is our readiness to see other people as subhuman and potentially dangerous. Third is replaceability. The killers need not worry about exterminating human creatures who may be of use to them, for, unless the extermination is total, they can be trusted to replenish themselves in another season, like cattle and grass. And with this view of replaceability goes the one that sees humans solely as groups or batches—one batch is as good as another—and never as made up of unique individuals. Finally is the appeal of the pure agency of killing, as contrasted with the pure passivity of being killed. The killer is under the illusion that he, as the dispenser of death—as the hooded figure with the scythe—cannot himself be mowed down by the scythe. He is above death. The psychology applies with even greater force to the group: horsemen charging across the field, swords slashing at fleeing foot soldiers, must feel an intoxicating rush of power and invulnerability.

I have given the killer's viewpoint. What about the victims? How do the inmates of a concentration camp, lined up and waiting to be shot by their Nazi executioner, see themselves and each other? To a surprising degree they share their executioner's view. Consider the fact that, even though the victims know their death is certain, they make no effort to retain a thread of their dignity with a gesture of protest, such as stepping out of line. Asymmetry of power reduces the victims, no matter who they once were, to nonentities in their own eyes. Here is another example. In the notorious Abu Ghraib prison in Iraq, the inmates were stripped naked and made to crawl, reduced to animals. Their military handlers never have to use force to produce, for their entertainment, a pyramid of writhing naked bodies. With a simple command the inmates move into position and kneel one on top of another. With a gloved hand handlers raise their bottoms up to the desire height and exposure and then cover their heads in plastic wraps so that they are not even animals, just bags of meat.[15] No killing ensued. It wasn't part of the game. Moreover, killing could seem anticlimatic, with power so effortlessly exercised.

The ease with which a man can lose his sense of self-worth and fall into the pit of self-abasement is a deeply disturbing psychological fact. Asymmetry of power doesn't have to be extreme for it to happen. All that is required is for it to seem implacable. Even in a democracy, as I noted earlier, a healthy young man may tremble and be on the verge of collapse in the presence of another man. Why? Well, the other happens to be a Kennedy. That unexpected encounter with a figure of prestige is apparently sufficient to make a man forget that he, too, is made in the image of God.

A moral law we all want to hold on to—and, indeed, we are likely to go mad if we don't—is that good follows good, evil follows evil. If as individuals or as society we do something truly good, we expect it to bear fruit in ways we anticipate, and, as a bonus, in ways we couldn't have anticipated. Something like this does happen: good deeds, if they are carefully thought through, do get good results, which may be lasting. What about evil deeds? Common sense tells us that, if we do something truly bad, we can expect lasting evil as consequence. Earth-scorching wars should produce a more or less permanent blight on the landscape. They certainly shouldn't produce prosperity! We humans can hardly be expected to learn from the past and morally improve if good can come out of evil.

So what does history tell us? Consider Alexander the Great (356–323 BCE). What kind of a man was he? Was he "great"? And, if "great," then in what sense, and did he earn it? Historian A. B. Bosworth concludes that Alexander was indeed "great." He was supremely gifted at killing! He spent much of his time at it. History books usually tell us that Alexander was a world conqueror, and so, of course, he had to kill. But he also had a noble vision, which was to mingle peoples and cultures so that the "brotherhood of man" could become a reality. To Bosworth, this fraternal universe was never in Alexander's mind. It simply came to pass. In Ptolemaic Egypt and the Seleucid East, the races did slowly and haphazardly mingle; Greek in these areas did become the lingua franca and so facilitated the exchange of ideas; Greek sculpture did strongly influence early Buddhist art; and, in Alexandria, a genuine cross-fertilization of Jewish and Greek literature did take place. Could these advances have happened without Alexander's world conquest?[16]

Another example of much good emerging from great evil was the establishment of the Mongol empire during the thirteenth century. The Mongols succeeded through a combination of organizational genius and ruthlessness. Skill in riding and fighting on horseback made them, individually, formidable, but far more crucial to their success was the creation of military machines made up of human and animal parts. In the name of efficiency, fighting units broke away from ancient kinsfolk alliances, took on all able-bodied, and adopted the decimal system of grouping—10, 100, 1,000, and 10,000. Mongol armies reduced whole cities in western Asia to rubble; the people who survived were rounded up and divided into batches for systematic eradication. As the Nazis extracted gold from the teeth of corpses, the Mongols disemboweled their victims to remove swallowed jewelry. In China, which formed the southern part of the Mongol empire, the conquerors at first considered wiping out the entire population, as they would brush and forest to make way for pasture land. They refrained only because Chinese officials persuaded them that they could gain more by systematically "milking" the population—that is, by taxation. How convenient it was to have millions of human cattle on hand that dependably yielded wealth without any need on the conquerors' part to invest in their care.

The evil committed by the Mongol hordes was such that one could justifiably wish them a bad end. Darker and more ethically dubious is the wish that the countries they overran should remain desolate as a permanent reminder of human wickedness. There was desolation, but it did not last. By the end of the thirteenth century, although some cities remained empty shells, others flourished, thanks, in part, to the trade routes the Mongols made safe. In Persia, the conquerors left high administration in the hands of talented locals: ethnically and culturally diverse groups worked and lived peacefully together to produce a vibrant, cosmopolitan society. In China, the Mongols, suspicious of the locals, gave high administration posts to foreigners. One unintended result was that the Chinese elite, who traditionally filled the bureaucracy, had time to cultivate the arts and literature, which flourished. It is ironic that the Mongols, who initially considered the Chinese population an undifferentiated mass to be removed, ended by creating a condition that promoted the rise of highly individuated individuals—artists and writers. In time, the Chinese even learned to appreciate the Mongols for uniting North and South, two parts of a country that had been divided for centuries. In short, after unprecedented destruction much that was good in culture and society emerged in merely two decades.[17]

ONLY GOD CREATES EX NIHILO

It is human to focus on the good and forget the evil that precedes it and that, in some sense, makes it possible. A reason for this is that we are makers of things, and in making—and not just in cooking, as I expatiated earlier—destruction necessarily precedes construction. Only God creates *ex nihilo*. Humans can only create out of something that already exists, which means there has to be an earlier destruction phase. To make even the simplest bench a tree must fall. In China, where the traditional building material was wood, the rise of mega-cities from the first century CE onward caused the removal of whole forests in the northern part of the country. Ironically, even the most genteel and civilized of arts—writing—could bring about devastation. To write, one had to have ink made from the soot of burnt pine. It was merely a matter of time—and that not long—before the busy brushes of the vast Tang bureacracy brought baldness to the T'a-hang Mountains of Shanxi and Hebei.[18]

Another difference between God and us is that God creates without stress and strain. We cannot avoid either. When successful, however, the human product can seem pure inspiration and carried out with godlike ease. Michelangelo's (1475–1564) "David" (1501–1504) makes us think that it just gracefully and perfectly stepped out of the Carrara marble. Musical compositions by Mozart (1756–1791) give the impression of effortlessness. We know that this wasn't true of either artist. Both had to toil over their creations.

Architecture, however, presents a different story and raises a moral issue that does not apply to smaller works. The architect, unlike (say) the painter or composer, gets credit for what he himself has not put up. That strenuous and dangerous work is done by laborers and artisans. In late sixth-century China, the spread of Buddhism prompted an orgy of construction. One ruthless official ordered the building of seventy-two temples. When a monk rebuked him for the suffering and deaths that such rapid construction could bring, he replied that posterity would see only the imposing results and know nothing of the men and oxen that had perished.[19] In seventeenth-century France, the Palace of Versailles was an architectural triumph, raised not only as a suitable stage for an absolute monarch, Louis XIV (1638–1715), but also to project an ideal of civilized society. To disguise the extent of the casualty, workmen injured and killed on the job were carted out at night.[20] Even today, large-scale construction may cause injury or death. Workers, for example, died in the course of building the World's Fair in Montreal in 1967. Free tickets were given to their spouses as partial compensation for their loss.

THE CALAMITY OF UTOPIAS

Despite human casualty and financial cost, buildings and public spaces rise up to be enjoyed by those who commissioned and used them and, in the long run, by the general public. Such is the story of the temples, churches, palaces, and great houses and parks of Europe and Asia. Now, my question is: What if a visionary potentate decides to produce not just new buildings and parks but a whole new society? The First Emperor of China, Qin Shi Huang (259–210 BCE), was such a visionary. He saw the horrors of a splintered world of contending kingdoms and sought to replace them with a unified empire. He did so by draconian means, through military conquest, by building a network of roads of standardized width that enabled soldiers and traders to move with minimal hindrance, by a highly centralized form of government, and by decrees aimed at achieving a uniformity of language, currency, and weights and measures. He also burnt books to ensure that no subversive ideas emerged to cause instability and chaos. The First Emperor's reign lasted only fifteen years. But did some good emerge from the excesses—the evil? Were there lasting legacies from the First Emperor's wars and depredations? One might say yes and point, architecturally, to the Great Wall, the road system, and other great engineering works, and, politically, to the recurrent dream of universal peace and stability.[21]

In our time, communism was to be the world's grandest blueprint for utopia. Its master builders, Joseph Stalin (1878–1953) and Mao Zedong (1893–1976), did not just seek to remake a social order and a landscape, which would have lacked originality, having been tried before at smaller scale by lesser potentates and master builders. The real challenge for them lay in changing human nature—in populating Earth with new men and women. That proved to be quite beyond the power, however great, of any dictator. What a dictator can create is uniformity: the uniformity of a landscape of collective farms and factories, the uniformity of people with no minds of their own, and, since mass-killing had to be a part of the technique, the uniformity of corpses.

Stalin and Mao obviously didn't learn from their predecessors Maximilian Robespierre (1758–1794) and Louise Antoine de Saint-Just (1767–1794). These French revolutionaries advocated a program that seemed to capture all that we today consider good in society. Its key word was *bienfaisance* (beneficence, happiness). In an upsurge of generosity and in the name of social justice, *bienfaisance* was to be extended to formerly marginalized groups, such as the poor, women, blacks, and children. The revolutionaries loved to love the people but all too often found them irritatingly unlovable. The result was growing intolerance and, in the end, a deep, unforgiving hatred for those who didn't comply or failed to measure up. A reign of terror followed, its one saving grace being that it didn't last long. Stalin's and Mao's reigns of terror didn't last long either, but, given modern techniques of domination, they were able to cower far more people and over a far larger territory.

What of the future? Humans have always disappointed dictators by their limited malleability and also by their great diversity. Genetic engineering may yet make humans easier to mold; as for diversity, much leveling has already been achieved with the time-tried methods of indoctrination and physical coercion, as well as with the newer psychological methods of marketing, backed by vast improvements in media technology. One source of power that goes against this trend and seems able to resist global leveling is group (ethnic, folk) culture and identity. The group has the political will to resist globalization by virtue of its own strongly shared values. But, as I noted earlier, it has its own defects: discouragement of individuality, suspicion of outsiders, and suspicion of all progress—social and material—that threatens to undermine the familiar and the known.

DIVIDED SELVES AND EVIL

I have raised the question of evil and spoken as if it can be sharply distinguished from good; moreover, I have also spoken in such a way as to imply that some people are good and others are not so good or bad. Of course, this is a gross simplification, We are all divided selves, acting quite different roles in the course of a single day. One of the sharpest role divides is between the biological and the social; the one crude, the other refined. One moment I strain over the toilet bowl, more animal than man, and the next I read *The New York Times* over Turkish coffee, one moment I line up with students at the urinal, and another I am the professor pontificating on humanist geography.

If I am unaware of these shifts, it is because my ability to function and my very sanity require that I am not. How can I lecture when I carry the image of my biological self into the classroom?

Forgetting one role as I move on to another is so critical to life that it may have a genetic basis. While this may be true, it is certainly also true that culture plays a part. It does so by segmenting a space: one type of space prompts one type of behavior; another type of space prompts another type of behavior. The shift from biological to social that I have given examples of is not, however, an ethical issue. Radical change in behavior within the social is or can be. In a Nazi concentration camp, an SS officer, a gentleman in his own quarters, can turn into a monster of arrogance and sadism the moment he steps into the inmates' barracks. Like others, I was shocked by the volte-face; but I now see it with a glimmer of understanding as an extreme instance of a common type of behavior, which is to act like different persons in quick succession with no sense that anything unusual has occurred.

Segmented space is a feature of advanced societies. In them, more than in simpler societies, people are encouraged to play roles. Role playing can corrode the integrity of character along the lines I have indicated. On the other hand, advanced society's practice of segmenting space also provided secluded areas, such as a quiet study, into which one can withdraw to ponder who one really is. How many people actually do so and how often? Very few and rarely. To reflect on the self is to take a risk, for it can lead to the unwelcome discovery that there is no core self or to a keen awareness of the world's malignancy and, what is not much better, its utter indifference. Should we, then, not use the mind introspectively? It seems a pity, for introspection is a unique capacity of the species that has taken the universe more than 14,000,000,000 years to produce and that is ours to exercise as individuals in life spans of touching brevity. Moreover, there is always the possibility that something good can come out of the effort. As a result of introspection, we may know better our proclivities and aversions, our weaknesses, or, more simply put, just our fundamental selfishness. It is when we allow such self-knowledge to haunt and taunt us that we can hope to be truly moral beings.[22]

CHAPTER 11

Indivudualism

N OW THAT I HAVE NARRATED the defects of human nature and human society, let me pause to emphasize certain key points before I take up the gifts with which humans are endowed and the achievements that have resulted with their use. One key point is individualism. It has come to connote selfishness. The word "individual" itself has a slightly negative meaning in that it suggests isolation— an island that is not part of the main. The word "ego" fares worse, immediately calling to mind "egoism" and "egotism," even though its psychoanalytic meaning of a state between the "id" and the "world" is neutral. In the extreme case, the ego seeks godlike powers over his or her fellows, reducing them to submissive non-entities. Short of that, the ego is in danger of losing its distinctiveness in a sea of egos, all striving for the same sorts of advantage. An alternative for the isolated ego is to join a powerful group, sacrificing individual identity for group identity. Satisfaction, then, lies in the group's sense of superiority over other groups, reducing them to subservience either for use or as quaint objects and playthings.

That the powerful want to use people as they would draft animals or beasts of burden is understandable, but why do they also seek in them a quality that might best be called exotic quaintness? The answer lies in psychology and aesthetics of power. Zoo directors like to have their zoos populated by a wide variety of animals. The ruler, for his part, likes his domain to have a rich variety of colorful, ethnic peoples—provided, of course, they fully recognize his authority. In both the Old and New Worlds, rulers have amassed strange-looking flora and fauna and, in the case of the Aztecs, even strange-looking humans in their gardens. These gardens were tokens of the rulers' wealth but, even more, of their world domination.[1]

What about the liberal rulers of America? They favor diversity, which can be interpreted in two ways: one is to their credit, the other much less so. The creditable interpretation is that the push of liberal rulers toward diversity represents one more step toward liberalization. It shows an increasing awareness of core human values in each and every vital culture and the belief that multiple cultures thriving in close proximity, rubbing against one another, can lead to innovations of benefit to all. The less credible—indeed, the dark—interpretation has three parts. One is economic exploitation. Ethnics and new immigrants are welcome, because they provide cheap labor, doing the work that many Americans who have risen in the world do not want to do. Two is the moral satisfaction of having "our little brown brothers" (though, of course, the expression is never used) under one's benign guidance. Three is a combination of economic motivation and aesthetic sensibility: ethnics, dressed in colorful costumes and offering spicy foods, are a tourist attraction. Ethnic neighborhoods and festivities bring in money, as do gardens and zoos that display rich assortments of flora and fauna.

I have spoken much about the individual, defending it against the charge of selfishness. It is time I give it a more positive description, but I seem unable to do so without sounding paradoxical: thus, the individual is a rooted being who cares about his or her hometown but also the world, one who likes to work alone but also with others for the common good, one who values her or his own life and is yet willing to put it at risk for a friend or an ideal. Any city worthy of the name can be counted on to have such citizens. They are people who form professional and amateur associations, the flourishing of which bespeaks a dynamic city. Association members do not band together to answer a threat or compete with a rival group, as clan-dominated urban neighborhoods have done and still do. Also, unlike guilds of the past, modern associations do not make a fetish of protecting trade secrets; rather, they seek to advance their own hobbies and enthusiasms. Their orientation is to the future, in contrast to the past orientation of tradition-bound communities, be they folk or ethnic.

What about political caucuses? They resemble tradition-bound communities in that they are formed to protect a group's special needs and interests rather than to advance society as a whole; they tend to be conservative rather than progressive. But there are exceptions, an outstanding example being the political caucuses that led to the founding of the United States of America. Groups of strong-minded individuals met in Philadelphia in 1776 to create a federal union out of the separate colonies so as to fight against an exploitative and predatory mother country, England. This step might make the union seem just a device against an external threat. But it was more than that. Its larger and higher purpose was decidedly forward-looking, namely, to make America into a new society, a "light upon a hill," a beacon to humankind.

Who can join? Here, again, there is an important difference between communities and associations. Communities have closed or restricted memberships: to belong one has to be born into one, have ancestors who were born into one, or have the same skin color. Associations, by contrast, have open memberships. All who are dedicated to stem-cell research and have the necessary skills are welcome. And the same goes for other interests and passions. In this regard, nation-states are communities rather than associations. Their ideology calls for the people to have common roots in the land, an ideology that is suspicious for outsiders. Again, America is an exception. People of different nationalities and of different social and economic class are welcome. Old communal prejudices, however, hang on. For a long time, America favored light-skin over dark-skin immigrants, Western Europeans to Eastern Europeans and Asians. Within the country, social and academic institutions discriminated against women and minorities. And there was the egregious blight of slavery. Nevertheless, these discriminations were so contrary to the original purpose and ideals, proclaimed with such eloquence by the nation's founders, that they eventually started to fade.

PART IV

Human Capabilities
and Potential

CHAPTER 12

What the Senses Can Offer

B OOKS WRITTEN UNDER THE RUBRIC "the humanities" seldom draw attention to sensory delights that are part of daily existence. It may be that the senses are neglected because the rewards they offer are not considered an achievement. Animals, after all, know similar sensory pleasures, though perhaps not to human heights. Of animals it may be said that living is pleasurable when the body is fit and the senses function well. Of humans something more needs to be said, which is the role of the mind and its products (art, dance, literature, music, and science) in making the body and the senses not just function well but come exuberantly to life.

The senses are the biological basis of our experiencing: their powers are our potential, their limitations our fate. Sketches of these senses, which I now give, stress their capabilities, with the view of stimulating the questions: "How have we or I benefited?" "How have other peoples benefited in other times and places?" "Little? Much?" "To what extent are the perceptual gains and enrichments in some people and their lack in others a consequence of culture and environment?"

And, last but not least, there are the practical questions: "How can we be taught to love and care for our environment—how can we be ecologically responsible—unless we perceive with all our senses, unless the forests and the prairies are, to us, not just a view, but also a sound and a fragrance?"

KINESTHESIA

Life is motion. Infants pump their legs, babies crawl, and toddlers—well—toddle. Young children climb trees and hang upside down on the branches, or they run, their little legs a whirl, like that of an egg-beater. Teenagers may train themselves to be athletes, and, whatever the sport, they are pictures of grace, delightful to watch not only because of the grace—the aesthetics of motion—but also because of our empathy with their energy and joy. Training is work and not in itself always pleasant. And yet it is done, willingly, since the earliest age. Consider the baby, an efficient crawler, so why does it struggle to stand up and walk, only to fall? It tries repeatedly until it succeeds, refraining from going back to the tried-and-true crawl so as to reach a level of achievement that accords with the baby's growing sense of dignity. The ultimate bodily grace is the dance—in the Western world, the ballet—in which the body in motion, punctuated by fleeting stillness, turns into kinesthetic art. But for the dancer it is more than just art, with its unavoidable hint of the static; it is the overcoming of body's inertia, the downward pull of gravity—in a word, freedom.

By standing up the baby challenges gravity. The accomplished dancer carries it to the extreme of which the human body is capable. Between them lies a world of social gestures and movements that defy not so much gravity—our materiality—as our animality. Much in the bringing up of children consists in teaching them how to act like people. To act like people every gesture and movement is to be appropriate to the occasion. Ideally, society is a dance, and every society has its own choreography that is passed down the generations. The difference between the dance as aesthetic display and society itself as dance is that the latter rests on an asymmetrical relationship of power: one bows to a superior and kneels to a despot, both being gestures of submission. Bowing, however, can be mutual and done in acknowledgment of each other's dignity. Respecting another in the form of gestures is what etiquette aspires to teach. The special appeal of etiquette in the Western world is that it is rooted in the doctrine that all humans are equal before God. This is why Louis XIV would make a point of removing his hat and bowing to the maid when they happened to meet in a palace corridor at Versailles. That gesture elevated the king as much as it did the maid. It is society as dance at its best. A general characteristic of the dance, as it is of ceremony or ritual, is that all parts—all roles—matter.

Aristotle (384–322 BCE) gave us the five senses of touch, smell, taste, hearing, and sight to correspond with the five elements of earth, water, air, fire, and the quintessence. So the number is quite arbitrary, and yet Western culture seems chained to them. Part of the problem is the vagueness of the word "sense." We have a sense of motion, or is it a feeling of motion? Is our ability to tell humidity a separate sense, or should it be included under "touch?" Do humans, like animals, have a sense of direction? And what about the geographer's sense of place?[1]

I will stay with the traditional five; moreover, I accept Western culture's privileging of sight and hearing—the two distant sensors. I do so because, although cultures differ in the sense or senses they emphasize, the general historical trend is to pay more attention to sight and hearing. And for good reason: humans are primarily visual animals, dependent on sight for orientation and a sense of control over objects; as for hearing, its role among humans is magnified by their possession of language—our most precise and subtle means of communication. In the Western world, one speaks of seeing God and of the ultimate bliss in the Beatific Vision, but one also speaks of hearing God and obeying His commands. Smell and taste appear to enjoy the least prestige among us moderns, even though they contribute as much, if not more, than hearing and sight to our sense of being alive and well. We neglect them because they come too close to our animal selves. As for touch, it, too, has been neglected, yet its importance to life's happiness and, for that matter, to life itself admits no doubt.

TOUCH

"A human being can spend his life blind and deaf and completely lacking the senses of smell and taste, but he cannot survive at all without the functioning of the skin," noted anthropologist Ashley Montagu (1905–1999).[2] Skin stimulation is necessary to the proper working of the digestive and eliminative systems. Mammals cannot live without such stimulation. But there is also pleasure. The young delight in snuggling up to their mother's bosom. Once they reach maturity, bodily contact—the tactile pleasure of mutual exploration—declines. We humans are the outstanding exception, for with us there is a resurgence of tactile pleasure in sexual foreplay and in sexual union itself. Extended sexual foreplay, as distinct from courtship rites, is characteristically human. All but a few animals forego or curtail that preliminary state, because to sustain it requires a degree of aesthetic distancing that animals do not have. Think how, in human foreplay, the hand moves from rumpled hair and firm pectorals to soft skin below the armpit, the muscled thighs, the knee's hard knob, registering all the while temperatures that range from the nose's dry, cool tip to the groin's tropical heat. In human sexual congress, skin slaps against skin, bone crushes bone, body heat intermingles with hot breath, hands and limbs grapple in a frenzy unmatched in any other animals, thanks to hairlessness, arms that hug, and hands that explore. We are right to feel sorry for chimpanzees whose thick coat of hair hinders cutaneous pleasure and for seals who lack limbs to embrace.

The original meaning of "luxury" is erotic and nothing but erotic. It is not so much sinking into soft, satin pillows and sheets as sinking into the soft, warm flesh of the beloved, not so much being wrapped in mink as being wrapped in strong yet tender arms. Luxury, thus, is a human universal, known to all, if only in the brief period when the baby has access to the mother's body. Outside this experience, however, tactile experience differs widely from people to people, depending on the environment and culture. What, after all, can hunters in the Arctic, gatherers in the tropical forest, farmers in mid-latitudes, and fishermen on Pacific islands have in common? What they have in common are not the specifics of tactile sensation—the attack of sharp cold in the Arctic, of sea spray on wind-blown islands, the sticky embrace of heat in the tropics, and such like—but rather an abstract quality, the at times brutal harshness they know in work, whatever that work is.

Harshness, then, distinguishes all traditional outdoor means of liveli-hood from office work in a modern environment. At first this would seem an improvement for us moderns, but deeper consideration shows it not to be the case. The human body apparently needs more than just gentle brushes with the environment to function well. One evidence is that we moderns seek harshness by flocking to the beaches to be scorched by the sun and to high mountains to be thrashed by wind and pelted by snow and sleet. Different cultures offer different solutions to the need. Finns find tactile challenge in their sauna, tak-ing delight in the shock of jumping from sweltering heat to a snow bank or cold lake; the Japanese nearly scald themselves in hot baths. D. H. Lawrence (1885–1930), in *Women in Love* (1920), envisaged the harsh delights of copulat-ing with vegetation. His hero took off his clothes "and sat down naked among the primroses, his legs, his knees, his arms right up to the arm pits, lying down and letting them touch his belly, his breasts." He saturated himself with their contact but in the end found them too soft. And so he looked for places where he could sting his thighs "against the living dark bristles of the fir-boughs" and clasp "the silvery birch trunk" to feel "its hardness, its vital knots and ridges."[3]

Just as, in the midst of nature, we forget the range of tactile sensations, except when they are sharp and penetrating, so we forget the range of tactile sensations offered by culture unless they are the ones we deliberately provide for or seek out, such as diving into a pile of cushions or into the searing heat of the sauna or sweat lodge. Out of mind are the flood of strokes, embraces, brushes, grazes, licks, and taps that contribute to our well-being. In our own culture, think of the hot bath, the cold shower, the rough texture of toweling, the coolness of bed sheets, the cuddling pressure of a sweater, the cushy sup-port of a thick carpet, the bumpy resistance of a cobbled walk. The list goes on and on, for everything in our material environment has a tactile quality, conveyed to us not only by direct contact, but visually. A glass coffee table next to a soft, leather sofa is a tactile—and not just visual—composition. The fact is obvious, yet we need to be reminded. We go the art gallery for a rewarding visual experience. Yes, but the experience cannot be purely visual, for, if it were, we would be quickly bored. Consider "The Leaping Horse" (1825), the famous painting by John Constable (1776–1832). It caters almost as much to touch as to the eye. Standing in front of it the viewer feels the warmth of the wooden fence, the squidgy wetness of the earth, the cushiony tangle of weeds and wild flowers, the coolness of the dark water sliding over a hidden ledge.

The human touch's extraordinary sensitivity is taken for granted. We don't pause in wonder that we need no special training to tell the difference between a smooth pane of glass and one etched 1/2500-inch deep or that, by merely running a finger over bond paper, flower petal, and polished wood, we can tell subtle shifts in temperature and texture. One reason for the neglect is that touch retains—more or less—its sensitivity over a lifetime, and so it differs from taste, smell, hearing, and sight, all of which suffer sharp decline as we age. The value of a capability is recognized in its unexpected loss. Although touch's sensitivity declines slowly with the onset of years, temporary loss is common enough and vividly registered; for example, driving a car with heavily gloved hands, trying to tie shoelaces with frozen fingers, and the "yakky" feeling we have when jam is accidently smeared over our fingers. With jam on them we lose touch with the world.

The need to touch begins with life. Infants are buccal explorers. Children feel impelled to touch. The very young hug soft, round toys. Older ones enjoy kneading and patting mud into pies. The older the children, the more they are likely to play with harder and sharper objects, though there appears to be a culture-induced gender difference: girls retain a liking for soft textures even as they grow into young womanhood; boys, for their part, turn to trucks and Lego sets. The result is that girls feel at home in domestic space, boys in the built environment of rectilinear lines, surfaces, and jutting corners. This gender difference is diminishing, but will it disappear altogether? Women have softer bodies; they touch and hug more. The intimate experience of nursing a baby is something men can never know. Women still do most of the household chores, which involve direct contact: they use their hands to smooth bed sheets, puff up pillows, sew curtains, knead flour, and wash dishes. Men still do most of the physical work outdoors, confronting those hard and resistant objects, not, however, directly but mediated by sharp, metallic tools, such as the shovel, pick, and pneumatic drill.

Cultural differences can be striking. To judge from novels, the Chinese dote on how things feel to the human skin. Is it cool and smooth like jade? Is it soft under pressure? Moral notes complicate the sensation. Jade symbolizes purity, and so, when a young woman's breasts are said to be like "warm jade," mixed signals are projected: she is desirable but also pure.[4] A Chinese proverb, no doubt of Taoist inspiration, declares that "warmth and softness are always better than straight and hardness." Better? Morally better? That idea is compromised by brothels being described as "lands of warmth and softness." Where there is no question of sex, contact with warm, soft materials can provide simple pleasure. A common practice at the better restaurants is to distribute warm towels before the food appears. Wiping one's hands and face with them is singularly refreshing.[5]

To most people, this predilection for warmth is natural. Objects warm to the touch and warm places, such as the kitchen or bedroom, evoke human warmth. As a term of praise, warmth is not, however, universal. The Chinese may compliment a girl by likening her to "warm jade," but to the Greeks the greater compliment is to liken her to "cold water." In Greek folk songs, "coldness" ranks with "flowers" in the evocation of pleasure. Lovers may be pictured as strolling among flowers or on snowy slopes. To Chinese and Western men, softness is desirable in women but not necessarily to Greeks, who might flatter a woman by describing her as straight and hard, like a slim cypress. Perhaps even stranger is their comparing their bedfellow, in a flight of adoration, to gold, crystal, or marble.[6]

Touch unites. "Keep in touch," we say, meaning "write or call me." Underlying this casual expression is the yearning to touch literally and to be touched. The ultimate tactile high is sexual congress. Mystics may find ecstasy in divine embrace, but, for most of us, it occurs, if at all, only during fleshly entanglement with another person. The sense of being an individual and isolated self disappears. Yet, paradoxically, sexual congress is, for most of us, also the only time we boldly assert our individuality—our entwined or dual self—against the world. Normally, we defer to the world's power and lures. In the urgency of sexual passion, they are easily shunted aside. No wonder rulers view sex with deep suspicion.

TASTE AND SMELL

To anthropologist Claude Lévi-Strauss (1908–2009), culture was "cooked" as distinct from "raw."[7] More than the use of tools, cooking differentiates us from other animals. Cooking thus unites us all, but it also differentiates us in that each human group has its own foods and its own ways of preparation. True, the same might be said of other cultural activities and products, but, whereas we may find another people's clothing and housing peculiar, we are not repelled by them as we can be repelled by what another eats, perhaps from the notion that, although we are not necessarily the way we dress, we are in some profound sense what we eat.

Humans do share certain food preferences. One is a fondness for meat. As omnivores we can survive without meat. Nonetheless, in all known cultures, meat ranks above vegetables. For dwellers along the Arctic fringe, there is no choice—there is only meat. For hunter-gatherers in tropical forests, there is a choice: plants may supply most of the nutrients, but a feast is hardly a feast without meat. In advanced societies, meat is a mark of prestige, for only the rich can afford it. Officials in ancient China carried the sobriquet of "meat-eaters." In a typical, well-to-do American household, meat is put on the plate first, then the vegetables—serious food followed by mere garnishing.

Meat, though an item of prestige, also reminds us that we are animals. One way to dodge the reminder is to show discrimination: the meat of only certain "clean" animals is eaten; that of others is "foul" and taboo. Another way, which I noted earlier, is to chop up the meat and cover it in sauces, turning the result into culinary art. But the ultimate step is to abstain from meat altogether and become a vegetarian. The cost in forgoing meat's unique flavors and textures is high, at least in the initial phase, but, to those who aspire to rise above animality and even above being merely *homme moyen sensuel*, the cost is compensated by the feeling that one no longer swells the pain in creation and that one has gained moral stature.

To say of someone that he has taste is a compliment A diner who declines a bottle of wine on the ground that it doesn't quite meet his standard is obviously a man of taste. Taste, however, is not confined to food and wine. We have extended it to the higher arts of painting, music, and literature. A well-educated man discriminates and can offer reasons for his preferences. William James (1842–1910) applies it even to the moral realm, saying that the purpose of education is to impart a taste for goodness, enabling one to recognize a good person when he sees him.[8]

Because of its hint of elitism, "a man of taste" is become somewhat tainted—still a compliment but an ambivalent one. As for "a man of smell," the expression, if used at all, immediately puts one's dander up. Strange that two senses so experientially close (what we call "taste" is mostly "smell") are worlds apart in meaning. Taste is limited to sweetness, saltiness, bitterness, and sourness. Humans favor sweet foods, and "sweet," in Western societies, carries a positive, moral meaning: babies and women are "sweet," as is also a man of gentle disposition. Salt enhances the flavor of cooked foods, especially vegetables, which would otherwise be intolerably bland. It has this power, even in small amounts. Jesus says of his disciples that they are "the salt of the earth." Though only a few, they nevertheless can transform the many. "Bitter" is the taste of poison, "sour" that of food gone bad. Both are uncomplimentary when applied to people.[9]

A lady complained to Dr. Johnson that he smelled. "No madam," he replied. "I am odorous, you smell." Often used interchangeably and imprecisely, both words "odor" and "smell" have strongly negative meanings. One is their association with moral turpitude—the fragrance of saints contrasted with the foul odor of sinners; two is their association with rottenness and death; three is the desire of humans, who stand upright and use their eyes to survey the world, to distance themselves from creatures that crawl and sniff their way through life; and four is smell's linkage to a primitive part of the brain that controls emotion, mood, and involuntary movements, such as breathing, a beating heart, and genital erection. The fragrance of food makes the mouth water; the musky odor of sex—the yeasty "baked bread" scent of the body—stirs sexual longing. Involuntary arousal may give pleasure, but it is not something that humans can be proud of.

Humans are proud of their free associations: women and men meet, because they have in common professional or intellectual interests. Odor has nothing to do with it. But odor does play a role in two fundamental, biological relationships: that between woman and man and that between mother and child. When a woman and a man fall in love, we say they have the right chemistry (the right odor—pheromone) for each other. A human infant prefers its mother's scent to that of any other woman. The mother, for her part, shows an amazing ability to identify her infant's bassinet by scent alone.[10] Attachment to odor continues as the child grows older: she still likes to snuggle up to her mother not only for her accommodating bosom and arms, but also for her familiar odors. Attachment by smell is carried over to material objects. The child holds on to her security blanket for its odor as much as for its texture. American children enjoy "sleep-overs," yet in a strange bed, after the excitement of pillow fights, they long for their own snug bed and its comforting odor. Adults don't like to admit it, but one reason why they hold on to old raincoats, slippers, and other personal belongings is their subtle stew of scents, endearingly their own, though meaningless and even repellent to others.

Odor, as I have noted, can cause various involuntary arousals and responses. One that has yet to be mentioned is its power to throw a person back into the past. I am not thinking here of a deliberate effort to recall the past, which can be disappointing, like "walking in shadow along the road where I once played under the sun," wrote Marcel Proust (1871–1922).[11] What I have in mind is involuntary and much more vivid.

Here is an example from personal experience. I returned to Sydney, Australia, twenty-three years after leaving it as a child, expecting the visit to be filled with nostalgia. This didn't happen, for Sydney had modernized almost beyond recognition. My own neighborhood had not, however, changed. The house I lived in, the beach and the playground nearby, all remained much the same. Still, I could not plunge back in time, as I had hoped: the sights held me firmly to the present until, quite unexpectedly, I caught a whiff of seaweed coming off the bay, and for a brief moment I was thrown back into my childhood.

Odor can evoke the past in us for a number of reasons, one of which is simply that our experience of it as a child and as an adult has changed little, in contrast to the different ways we organize our visual field in the same period. Sight markedly expands and matures over time. Not so—or less so—smell. True, one learns to appreciate new scents as one gets older: the range increases, but the keenness of appreciation declines. It declines, yet retains the power to work its magic on memory.

Let me turn now to odors in the environment. They have deteriorated during the last 5,000 years, a consequence of ever greater crowding. Hunters and herders who roamed the open spaces had the best. Once agriculture took over and people lived in ever more densely packed quarters, bad odors started to accumulate, reaching a peak in the urban slums. Odor, no matter how strong and noxious upon first encounter, fades after a short period of immersion. People adjusted to foul air as they did its source—the blood and offal, mud and filth that overflowed the gutters. In European towns, the well-to-do only became sensitive to odors of putrefaction when, during the seventeenth century, they considered them the cause of sickness. Rather than promote hygiene and declare war on filth, they tried to combat foul odor with good odor: that is to say, to fumigate houses and streets with flowery scents, a procedure no more successful than when they doused perfume on their ill-smelling bodies.

Progress in hygiene was slow. The water closet, invented early in the seventeenth century, remained rare two centuries later, though it did, in time, play an important role in ridding households and neighborhoods of their most repulsive fumes. Improvements in hygiene took a notable step forward during the eighteenth century when urban planners, influenced by the revival of classicism with its aspiration toward geometric clarity, favored the construction of straight and broad streets, in sharp contrast to the winding mazes inherited from the Middle Ages. Through these wide streets cleansing winds could pass. During the nineteenth century, this geometric ideal found its culminating expression in the radiating streets and avenues of Paris. It was also in this period that major European cities built a subterranean world to service the world above, an important component of which was an elaborate and efficient system of sewers.[12]

Increasing sensitivity to bad odor has had an unexpected social effect: it sharpened class distinctions and heightened prejudice against the "lower orders." In Europe, for centuries the rich stank almost as much as the poor, which could explain why the two classes didn't mind sharing the same quarters and even the same bed. Once the rich benefited from improved hygiene and learned to appreciate cleanliness, they attributed bad odor—harbinger of disease and death—solely to the poor, as though it were their innate and indelible characteristic. Cities henceforth became sharply divided into rich and poor quarters, with the latter located downwind from garbage dumps and smelly factories.

New olfactory standards required that upper-class men be odorless, except for the faint whiff of a Cuban cigar trapped in the folds of their elegant tuxedo. Upper-class women sought to distinguish themselves from other women, even those of their own class, by applying a drop or two of expensive perfume behind the ears. Rising individualism plays a part behind this ideal. Each woman or man wants to be someone of special distinction. A woman is stunned and humiliated if, at a party, she finds herself wearing the same dress as another. As for the men, even though they all wear the tuxedo, they are nevertheless aware that not all tuxedos are created equal. For all that, the true individual is not in the outward clothing; it is, rather, in his scent, which emits from the depth of his being, where his soul is located.

American cities strive to be odorless. Only their ethnic enclaves can have a distinctive effluvium and still be respectable. White Americans go there for exotic foods and appreciate the aromas that drift onto the streets from food stores and restaurants. After taking in the stimulations of a poorer world they return to their odorless, glistening, glass-and-steel towers, swept streets, and manicured lawns, in which all signs of the downward curve of organic life— dead leaves, birds, and squirrels—are removed. The modern city caters primarily to sight, the sensory organ that flatters our intelligence and makes us feel in control. Even at the market's meat counter and in public rest rooms odor is out of bounds.

Some subtle aromas are, however, welcome in the city: for instance, those that escape onto the sidewalk from the open doors of a bakery, coffee shop, flower shop, leather-goods store, and used bookstore. They are a delight to passers-by, a delight registered subconsciously rather than in critical appreciation. Stronger odors may not be pleasant, but they give character to place. A map of scents of Manhattan shows their extraordinary range and pungency: everything from Central Park's spicy-lemony pink flowers, subtle sun-drenched lime, mulch, dead leaves, and runner's sweat, to Midtown's new clothes, salty Armani leather, sporty perfume, popcorn, fries, exhaust, and horse urine, to Chinatown's moldy newspapers, fresh fish, dried mushrooms, dried shrimp, day-old snails, lunch from trapdoor, dog feces, garbage, and soiled pavement. And this is just a small sample! What I have said earlier about ambivalence toward odor remains true. We in America are not proud of this particular sensorial plenitude. Chambers of Commerce never advertize it.[13]

What about the scents of nature? They were suspect in eighteenth-century Europe, especially those that emanated from the bowels of the earth. Quarries were to be avoided, for they exuded a "metallic vapor that attacks the nostrils and the brain." The countryside was unhealthy, for it was where soils were turned over, releasing "morbific vapors." Virgin soils were the most dangerous. Their cultivation was believed to account for the fevers suffered by New World colonists.[14] Eventually, a complete change of attitude came about when attention turned away from Earth's soil, marshes, and fissures to the cleansing air, especially that which came off the mountains and the sea and the scents of trees and flowering plants. These were valued during the nineteenth century, because they were thought to be health-giving and, during the twentieth century, for the same reason but also, increasingly, as a respite from the boring odorlessness of the built environment. Who nowadays would not feel a lift of the spirit at the aroma of grass, sun-baked wood or rock, plowed soil, fir and pine, or piñon and eucalyptus?

Even when Europeans learned to appreciate nature's fragrances, few attempts were made to reproduce them close to the city or indoors. By the early modern period, gardens rose to the highest visual splendor, but they were strikingly deficient in fragrance. Only the bowery, where the ladies congregated to embroider, was designed for it. The Chinese were different. They might deliberately surround a building with plantings so their scent could penetrate the interior with the help of either a natural or fan-induced breeze. The Palace of Coolness, built in thirteenth-century Hangzhou, is an outstanding example. The palace itself is fragrant, being made of pinewood. Several ancient pine trees stand in front to add to the aroma. An artificial waterfall cascades into a lake covered with pink and white water lilies. In the courtyard surrounding the palace are hundreds of urns containing jasmine, orchids, flowering cinnamon, and other rare shrubs. A windmill fans them so their fragrances can waft into the palace's great hall.[15]

As I consider this description of the Palace of Coolness, I almost wonder whether the fragrance may be too strong for me. Cultures differ in the odors they prefer, but, perhaps in all, excess is avoided. We speak of beatific vision and of heavenly music and do not easily imagine an upper limit in the beauty beyond which lie revulsion and pain, but of fragrance we can easily so imagine. Why is this the case? Is it because pleasure in odor is like pleasure in eating and sleeping, in which animal needs and indulgences have a clear upper bound?

HEARING

Most people consider loss of sight a greater catastrophe than loss of hearing. We have only to close our eyes to be plunged instantly into darkness; whereas, if we plug our ears, the silence that ensues feels peaceful, as a city is peaceful, its noises muffled, after a heavy fall of snow. Moreover, absence of sound can enhance visual acuity: we focus better, and the world seems more sharply defined, when it is not blanketed by diffuse sounds. Soundlessness, however, begets a feeling of deadness. In my soundproof, high-rise apartment, I stand by my window and look down and out on the city. I see buildings and streets with people and cars moving on them. I can see that the city is alive, but I know it—I feel it with my whole being—only when I throw the window open and street noises pour in.

Of the sounds in our environment by far the most important and, therefore, the one to which we are most sensitive is the human voice. We become human by listening to others speak and learning to speak. We become participating members of a community through speech, with its useful information and, just as vital, its messages of concern, encouragement, and love. Those deprived of hearing are isolated from a reassuring cocoon of voices, mixed with other sounds that are almost as familiar and reassuring—the soft night noises, as John Updike put it, of "a mother speaking downstairs, a grandfather mumbling in response, a kettle whistling in the kitchen, cars swishing past."[16]

In our frantic, noise-filled modern world, silence is considered highly desirable—a life-restoring experience. But silence also signifies death. Silence is of the tomb. For long periods nature's silence—in the absence of wind—broods over ice plateaus and deserts. In the mid-Atlantic, sailors in sailing ships dreaded the preternatural calm that settled over them under subtropical high pressure. For days on end nothing stirred, and quietude so reigned that all the sailors could hear were the quotidian noises on the ship and, perhaps in dread, their own heartbeat. European travelers, habituated to the rustling noises of broad-leaved forests, were stunned by the quiet of the North American grasslands. Most frightening and oppressive of all is the silence of outer space.

It was not always thus. Quite the contrary. For more than a millennium space beyond the orbit of the moon was believed to be filled with celestial music.[17] Shakespeare certainly thought so. "Sit Jessica. Look how the floor of heaven is thick inlaid with the patines of gold." That's just the visual beauty. There's also the beauty of sound, for "There's not the smallest orb which thou behold'st but in his motion like an angel sings."[18] When Blaise Pascal (1623–1662) looked up at the night sky, what did he see? Not heaven's floor inlaid with patines of gold. And he didn't hear any music. Instead, he was confronted by empty space and an eternal silence that frightened him. Silence is rejection, indifference, and death.[19]

Silence in outer space is total. Not even the collision of galaxies makes a sound that can be heard by human ears. On Earth, silence is more the exception than the rule. Perhaps, for this reason, we tend to take nature's sounds for granted and fail to acknowledge their range in volume and variety. And what is the range in volume? Everything from the gentle rustling of leaves to the roar and screech of tornadoes and hurricanes and thence to the cataclysmic blast of volcanoes, the loudest ever recorded being that of Krakatoa in 1883, which could be heard 3,000 miles away. Variety is just as remarkable. Think of pleasing sounds, such as rain sighing through a needle-leaf forest, waves lapping on a lakeshore, and pigeons cooing in a misty morning; think of less desirable sounds, such as the ceaseless roar of waterfalls, the nonstop sighing of the trade winds, the bursts of thunder, the loud cracks of ice breaking off near the poles, and, among the animal noises, the din of insects and frogs, the chatter, call, and bloodcurdling scream of monkeys in tropical forests, the cry of wolves and the howl of loons in northern forests, the unceasing buzz of cicadas (the loudest of insects), and the warbling of crickets in Australia.[20]

Given the fact that much of nature's sounds are indiscriminate and jumbled together, long persistent quiet broken by clear, ringing notes provides the keenest pleasure to the human ear. Russians, perhaps because they seldom live far from wide-open spaces, are especially appreciative. It is almost a cliché for Russian writers to include a scene in which, over the vast, snow-muffled steppe, riders warmly bundled up in their troika rejoice in the sudden trilling of a lark, dropping silvery notes on them, like beneficence, from the airy heights.

Is such appreciation known to pre-modern and pre-literate peoples? They are without doubt keenly sensitive to the sounds of nature, which can be warnings of danger or messages from spirits. But do they ever listen solely for their beauty? One people apparently do: the Mbuti hunter-gatherers in northeastern Congo. They are familiar with the many animal noises of the tropical rainforest, but only the song of a particular bird is thought to have supernatural beauty. The rarity of auditory aesthetics in pre-modern and folk cultures may have to do with its not serving a social purpose or practical need. People who do have such an aesthetic are those who do not have to worry about their livelihood: the Mbuti, for example. Their confidence in their food supply lies in their rich, natural environment. More generally, advanced societies have such confidence. In them attentiveness to the beauty of sound, including nature's, is common. Less common, though still of frequent occurrence, is an individual's willingness to attend to the quality of one sound to the exclusion of others—*this* bird's song, the rustling of *those* leaves, the babbling of *that* brook. Such willingness can make one feel isolated, at odds with one's group. In pre-modern and folk communities, neither pure aestheticism nor individuality, both of which are luxuries of affluence, find a recognized place in their scale of values.

A human being's voice is the organ with the largest number of moving parts, which explains why it is unique. We more readily mistake a face than a voice, for the one changes with hairstyle and age, while the latter remains much the same over decades of time. The test of this assertion, however, has become common only in modern times with the wide use of the telephone. The first word heard over the telephone not only identifies the person, but even his mood.[21] In addition to the sound of the voice, the content of what is said can also be highly distinctive. We are generally unaware of this distinctiveness, because, for most practical purposes of life, we need to act as a group, which means that we need to see ourselves as much alike. Seeing human individuals as different, each with a unique voice and a distinctive world-view, is another luxury of advanced societies.

MUSIC

Nature's sounds are, at one extreme, terrifying, and, at the other extreme, merely pleasant. Why the asymmetry? Why is the positive end of the response only pleasant? Why can't nature's sounds be deeply moving rather than just terrifying or piercingly beautiful rather than just attractive? A bird's song, however agreeable after a rain shower, just doesn't have the power to elevate us to another level of being as can a brilliantly multi-hued sunset or the ethereal dancing lights of aurora borealis. For humans, nature's inability to provide sublime sounds is compensated by music.

Music's basic rhythms are those of the body—the breathing in-and-out, the heartbeat, and the swinging of arms and legs when one walks. Slowing the rhythm means relaxation; speeding it means excitement and martial vigor. Tied with bodily rhythms, music enhances an individual's sense of life. It also has the power to bind the group. When people sing in syncopated beat, with eyes half-closed, it is though they have become one large, organic whole.

Given this biological grounding and the biosocial needs it serves, we shouldn't be surprised to find that traditional or folk music is much alike everywhere and that it has changed little over time. Consider two very different kinds of music made a thousand years apart and for very different purposes: the Gregorian chant of the Middle Ages and hard rock of our time. For all their differences the two musical modes produce a similar social effect, which is the loss of the self in the whole. In regard to Gregorian chant, the effect is aided by the church's stone walls, which absorb high frequencies and produce long reverberations, with the result that chants appear to come from no particular point to bathe the congregation in warmly flowing rhythms, making it feel "one." As for rock, the electronically amplified boom on stage overcomes the audience, reducing it to a sweating, gyrating mass, in which the sense of being an isolated individual is blissfully drowned.

A musical innovation unique to the West, from the mid-sixteenth century onward, is to expand greatly the range of both intensity (loudness) and frequency (pitch). In a single composition, the sound may be so soft as to be barely audible and so loud as to be on the verge of causing pain. As for pitch, it ranges from bass, whose low rumble is more felt than heard, to a note that is piercingly high and seems to rise to the sky or reach the far horizon. A consequence is the opening up of acoustic space, a move that reminds us of the opening up of visual space in landscape painting. Music attains, as it were, "perspective" just as painting did earlier. With this new development, rather than being submerged in sound, wrapped in it, one stands a little apart to listen.[22]

Did people in pre-modern communities listen quite this way? I have already concluded that the answer is "no" in regard to nature's sounds. I believe the answer is also "no" in regard to music. In pre-modern communities, rituals and songfests involved everyone. Those who couldn't participate for reasons of age or infirmity might still want to move their bodies, stump their feet, and hum along to the extent they could. Absent was the category "listener." True listening, then, is a phenomenon of large, complex societies, for only in them is standing aside for the purpose of critical judgement and appreciation a commonplace, and only in them is the individual talent openly recognized and rewarded. I can imagine Roman connoisseurs of the good life savoring, after dinner, the beautiful singing voice of a slave or of a Chinese official pausing on his way home enthralled by a flutist playing by a mountain stream and later telling his friends of his remarkable find. In other words, a listening culture has to accept—even approve of—a certain degree of distancing and isolation.

Popular music affirms the group. Classical music, from the end of the nineteenth century on, is increasingly wary of easy group affirmations, being more concerned with what an individual is capable of experiencing as one follows one's life-path. Witness the two popular classical genres—the sonata and symphony. Both feature separate movements: apparently three to four of them are necessary to capture a self's varying moods. Or, to put it in temporal terms, each movement is part of a narration, revealing a different stage in a person's life. If to appreciate a human individual requires that one attend to more than just a mood or even a period in life, so to appreciate a sonata or symphony one can't just pick a catchy tune or even a whole movement but must follow the narrative line of the entire work.

Music is nonetheless social. In early modern Europe, it served both the official church, elevating the tone of its rites, and society, imparting a sheen of sophistication to the drawing-room coterie. Today, classical concerts are well attended, but one suspects that some people are there to be seen as much as to listen. Symphonies are occasions for the socially ambitious to dress up, meet the right people, and advertize their high, cultural taste. Music's own reason for being is thus sidetracked. And what is music's—that is, classical music's—reason for being? Is it to express a range of emotions, a surpassing sense of beauty and good, beyond what words and gestures and, for that matter, folk and popular music can express? At the highest level of achievement, classical music has the feel of an intimate conversation between two individuals and a mass celebration of our common humanity.[23]

To give a personal example, when I listen to J. S. Bach (1685–1750), I feel as though we have grown up together, went to the same school, worshiped the same God in the same church. How else can he know my deepest feelings and desires? Yet nothing can be further from the truth. Bach and I are worlds apart in every conceivable way: he is a German of the eighteenth century, a *pater-familias*, a man of enormous mental and physical vigor, a musician of unsurpassed genius; I am a Chinese of the twentieth century, a life-long bachelor, a shy man of low vitality, a geographer of moderate achievement. Bach spoke the musical language of his time. Why would it be able to engage my heart in ways that my mother tongue and musical tradition cannot? Listening to the andante and larghetto sections of compositions by Bach, Mozart, or Beethoven (1770–1827), I feel we are engaged in intimate conversation. And yet multitudes in different parts of the world respond to their music in the same personal way. Experiencing great music, then, is something of a paradox. What feels like a tête-à-tête, a transaction between two individuals at a specific time and place, is also communal and universal in scope and reach.

SIGHT

"Above all others we love the sense of sight," so Aristotle wrote, and I think most of us would agree, for we depend on sight more than on the other senses to navigate the world and appreciate its infinite variety. What we don't realize is that we use only a tiny fraction of our visual potential. Environment itself can impose severe limits. The Inuit, living along the Arctic coast, see little else but white and gray most of the year. How strange that they should live without the warm colors that we of mid- and tropical latitudes take for granted. Were an Inuit to visit the tropics, would it be like how I felt when I first switched from black-and-white to color TV, surprised that I could do without colors for so long? And what of Pueblo Indians, who live in the midst of the bright mineral hues of the Southwest, not knowing the opalescent grays and dull browns of Americans living in the humid East and vice versa?

Besides color, environments differ in such general characteristics as verticality and horizontality, openness and crowding. The Tuareg of the Sahara rarely see a vertical, except for the occasional dust devil that drifts across their path. By contrast, the Mbuti live in a crowded verticality of trees and rarely see a horizontal. Environment that constrains also sharpens. The Inuit are well-known for seeing all sorts of subtle variation in snow, and the hunter-gatherers of the Kalahari desert can find tiny shoots of edible plants invisible to outsiders. More remarkable still is that certain tribesmen known to ethnographers and certain sailors known to historians of navigation can see the planet Venus in broad daylight.[24]

Another constraint on sight is the lack of words to draw attention to its subtle powers of discrimination. Take color, again. Some small hunting-gathering bands have no color terms or only basic ones of black, white, and red. As the size and complexity of a human group increase, more terms are added to the group's vocabulary. The addition is in sequence: white, black, and red are followed by green, yellow, blue, brown, purple, pink, orange, and gray, to make up a total of eleven. Why just these colors? The answer is that, unlike the innumerable hues that the eyes can discern, only eleven matter in most people's practical and emotional life, only eleven—and especially the first six—carry strong symbolic resonance.[25] For evidence, consider the colors used in national flags. Nations are free to use any color they like, yet, without any sort of consultation, the overwhelming majority choose just the first six. Somehow the rest are not regarded as suitable.

A flag's colors, like a national motto or slogan, must have a certain blatancy. That is precisely what artists want to avoid. Their aim is subtlety and nuance. Of the eleven basic color terms, artists—especially those of the Impressionist school—may prefer the last six in the sequence. Writers also have their preferences. G. K. Chesterton has famously rhapsodized over gray. It was, for him, the color of possibility—the color that "always seems on the eve of changing to some other color; of brightening into blue or blanching into white or bursting into green and gold." But gray's chief glory lies in that, as background, "every color appears unusually beautiful. A blue sky can kill the brightness of blue flowers. But on a gray day the larkspur looks like fallen heaven; the red daisies are really the red lost eyes of day; and the sunflower is the vice-regent of the sun."[26]

Chesterton's preference is only likely to receive a hearing in a sophisticated society where an individual's eccentricity is valued. If Chesterton opted for gray, Rainer Maria Rilke (1875–1926) opted for blue and so on. Individual taste is a badge of pride. A sophisticated society is by its nature discriminating. Yet it can also deliberately go to the opposite extreme of total acceptance. Nothing is unworthy of regard. Gerard Manley Hopkins (1844–1889) found beauty in the urinal, provided it was "frosted in graceful sprays."[27] Gustave Flaubert (1821–1880) was stopped in his track by "a drop of water, a shell, a hair."[28] Eugène Delacroix (1798–1863) paused for the garden slug and not just the noble lion. Robert Rauschenberg (1925–2008) paused for the lowly urban scene—the patterns and textures of decaying walls with their torn posters and patches of decay. We non-artists may be surprised, even repelled. Yet, in time, these seeming eccentricities can infiltrate our own appreciation of the world around us.[29]

The aesthetic posture of non-discrimination in the art world overlaps with the religious doctrine that everything in God's creation is worthy of notice, if not adoration, that anything that exists at all is a miracle. St. Francis of Assisi (c. 1182–1226) was famously all-embracing in his love of sun, moon, rock, flowers, birds, insects, bees, wolves, ass, oxen, pigs, worms, reptiles, and lepers. Zen Buddhism takes a similar view. Since Buddha is everywhere, what place is not holy—what place is not worthy of notice and respect? The story goes that a monk is admonished by his superior for spitting in the temple. The monk's remonstrance, "But, sir, where can I spit that is not Buddha?"

Individuals differ in what they see and choose to see; likewise, groups and communities. When groups and communities become large and complex—that is to say, civilizations—they share a high regard for one aspect of nature—the stars. Stars define civilizations, as no single natural feature on Earth—tree, rock, stream, or mountain—can be said to define cultures. In the stars, the ancients of Meso-America, the Middle East, and China found inspiration to free themselves from bondage to Earth. Their skyward turn was most vividly manifest in cosmic ceremonial centers and geometric cities. The ancients believed that stars influenced human affairs. They, therefore, had a practical reason for treating the stars with respect. There were, however, exceptions to the lure of mere practicality. If the Hebrews turned admiringly to the stars in heaven, it was because they were God's handiwork and declared His glory (Psalm 19). As for the ancient Greeks, suffice it to quote Anaxagoras (c. 500–428 BCE), teacher of Socrates (469–399 BCE), who answered the question, "To what end are we born?," with "to behold the sun, moon, and sky."[30] During the late Middle Ages, Dante (1265–1321) pictured himself emerging, with Vergil (70–19 BCE), from the pits of hell to behold "the lovely things [the stars] the skies above us bear."[31] In Shakespeare's *The Merchant of Venice* (1596–1598), Lorenzo says to his beloved, "Sit, Jessica. Look how the floor of heaven/ Is thick inlaid with patinas of bright gold." The lovers can see the stars, but most people, in their "muddy vesture of decay," cannot.[32] We moderns are even worse off, for not only do we remain vestured in muddy clothes of decay, but we have also dimmed the "patines of bright gold" by the glare of city lights. To our credit, many of us consider such dimming a desecration.

Next to the sky in human visual scope is the landscape. Only two civilizations—European and Chinese—have learned to see and admire an expansive composition of natural and artifactual features. This can be surprising to us, so used are we to the idea of landscape. Yet we know for a fact that neither of the two other great civilizations—Hindu and Islam—have conceived it. Once conceived, landscape finds quick acceptance. From China the art of landscape depiction spread to Korea, Japan, and southeast Asia; from Europe it spread to all parts of the world where European civilization had an influence. An example of the reach of this art is its adoption by Australian aborigines. Their paintings of the harsh yet weirdly beautiful scenes feel so authentic—so in character with the sort of people they are—that it is a shock to realize their alien source.[33]

As for Europe and China, they embraced landscape art only after having passed through a succession of earlier phases, devoted to bounded objects, such as human figure or face, a building, tree, flower, or animal. Landscape is an abstraction, its borders quite arbitrary; it is also an organization of nature at a supra-human scale. A taste for it can happen only after the people have reached a certain level of self-confidence vis-à-vis "wild" nature, which, in China, was around 1000 CE and, in Europe, some four centuries later. True, landscape art already made an appearance in Roman villas, and that in itself is revealing, for Roman villas were architectural showpieces—symbols of power and control. Nonetheless, only much later—at the dates indicated—did landscape painting begin to infiltrate and even dominate the aesthetic imagination.

European and Chinese landscape paintings have much in common—the same basic composition of vertical and horizontal elements (though the elements themselves differ) and the same sense of space opening out invitingly into the distance. But their differences are just as striking. One difference is simply the result of the medium used—predominately oil in the West and watercolors in China. The result is that Western landscapes, even those of J. M. W. Turner (1775–1851), feel heavier and more grounded than Chinese landscapes. Robinson Jeffers's complaint that rocks in Chinese landscape painting "have no weight" may have more to do with the medium than with—as Jeffers (1887–1962) believed—morals.[34] A second difference is in attitude towards mountains. The verticals in Chinese landscape are the towering mountains; in the West, they are more likely to be buildings, trees, and human figures until well into the nineteenth century. True, jagged peaks appear in "The Virgin and Child with St. Anne" (1510), the painting by Leonardo da Vinci (1452–1519), but they are in the background: St. Anne remains the dominant vertical.[35] A third difference is one of technique. Europeans developed the single perspective, the ideal of presenting what the eyes see from a single standpoint. But why from a single standpoint? The answer is Europe's greater interest in the individual. In the early modern period, not everyone is an individual, only the powerful. The potentate in his high chair commands a view, and that view—his view—is a landscape.

The word "landscape" itself is revealing. It is made of two parts: "land" and "scape." Land is where communities are located; it has no view and no individuals. By contrast, "scape" comes to mean the view or prospect of the potentate from his privileged standpoint. The Chinese make no such distinctions. Their use of multiple perspectives denies the single, commanding view. And yet, once the Chinese learned the West's conception of landscape, they, too, favored the single perspective. They apparently cannot resist following the West's trend toward greater individualism.[36]

West and East also differ in their treatment of the seasons and of light and shadow. The seasons figure prominently in Chinese and Japanese paintings but far less so in those of Europe. Why? It may be that, unlike Europe, the cosmic model continues to dominate East Asia, and it does so because of East Asia's more enduring dependence on agriculture. Rather than the seasons, Europeans have turned to the more evanescent times of the day—to how light plays on the surface of a pewter jar, to how the early morning sun burnishes hilltops and evening stars make fairy lights dance on ocean waves. Do Asian artists lack the technique to do justice to the subtleties of light, or is the cause more fundamental—the lack of a theology of light? Both play a role, but I believe the latter is more important, for, if Asians had a theology of light, it is hard to believe they would not have come up with the necessary painterly skills. The first verses of Genesis and the first verses of the Book of St. John are all paeans to light—to God as light, to Jesus Christ as light. True, Buddhists also seek light or illumination, a metaphor for wisdom that is hard to avoid. Still, light doesn't have quite the prominence in Buddhist doctrine, myth, ritual, and architecture that it does in the Judeo-Christian tradition.[37]

THE CAMERA

What we see and how we portray it change over time. In most parts of the world, the change is slow. In the West, it has been fast, thanks in large part to technological innovations, the most important of which is the camera. Since its invention during the early part of the nineteenth century, the camera has subtly altered our sense of reality. Curiously, the alteration is more in our relation to time than to space; or rather to space—and objects in space— as the result of a different feeling for, and attitude toward, time. Let me explain.

A common, even universal, human experience is of people, events, and scenes all slipping into the past or about to do so. A child's smile is a heart-warming image that we wish to retain, but it quickly fades. Our friend gets on his horse for a long journey, we say good-bye, he turns his face, and almost immediately that beloved image loses its sharpness, not to be regained until the next meeting, which may be years away, and he will have changed. A patch of Earth's surface—a landscape—stays put, and we think we can always go back to it. But can we? What if it is far off? Even if we are able to return, will not *we* have changed and so also the landscape?

Memory is, in any case, unreliable. Poor Wordsworth (1770–1850)! He was born just too soon for the camera. As we can see from the following complaint, he could have used one in his tour of the Alps: "Ten thousand times in the course of this tour have I regretted the inability of my memory to retain a more strong impression of the beautiful forms before me, and again and again in quitting a fortunate station have I returned to it with the most eager avidity, with the hope of bearing away a more lively picture."[38]

Today, tourists will not want to go to exotic places without a camera. They take pictures, and, if by accident they do not come out, it is as though the tour itself has been cancelled. One possible reason for this attitude is the photograph's special reality status. As captured on camera, a child's shy smile or a late-afternoon landscape is not just a representation, as a painting would be, but rather a presentation that contains a trace of reality, that trace being the impact of refracted sunlight on chemically treated film or on the sensors of a digital camera. A father looking at a photo of his daughter feels as though he is holding a bit of her substance and not just her image. Primitive men who do not like their photos taken may not be so backward after all. They rightly suspect that not only their image or soul, but even a bit of their substance is stolen.

There are other differences. When we look at a painting, we don't ask, "What lies beyond the picture frame?" With a photograph, we often do: we take for granted that a world lies beyond, just as when we look at a scene we assume that the world doesn't stop at the edge of our peripheral vision.[39] A landscape painting is, thus, more contained than a landscape photograph or field of vision, and for this reason alone it is considered by some to be more an art, if one had to choose between the two.

And this is not all. The camera, because of the ease it captures a scene and, perhaps also, because it is more portable than the unwieldy equipments of a landscape artist, encourages seeing as an act of freedom. This is even more true of the modern movie camera, which can be mounted on a crane that is capable of rising to varying heights and of swinging around, thus allowing the camera to register scenes quite unfamiliar to the person on the ground. Having watched many movies, I am accustomed to seeing places and people from a lover's close-up to the distant view of a bird in flight, altering from one to the other, and I would be bored if I can have only the static, earthbound human standpoint and angle.

Let me give an example of this novelty, one which we nevertheless quickly get used to and accept as part of our normal visual experience. In the film, *Providence* (1977), directed by Alain Resnais (b. 1922), the last scene is one of family reconciliation. The father, celebrating his seventy-eighth birthday, has invited his estranged son, daughter-in-law, and friends to lunch at his garden. They sit around the table, eat, and chat genially. The camera records this scene at ground level. It is what the actors see—what any group of people would see if they happen to have lunch outdoors. But then the crane lifts the camera into the air and swings it around so that it captures for the movie-goer images of the sky and treetops in a whirl and next lowers it to the ground level to record servants clearing the table. The end.[40]

What Resnais and his camera man have done may be dismissed as a trick, clever but way beyond normal human experience. So let us consider seeing as we normally do. We see objects that stay put, and we see objects in motion. Seeing motion—and not just seeing it, but also feeling and savoring it—is a challenge, one that the movie camera helps us to meet. It does so, in the first place, by catering to our desire. Early movies make a point of showing "crowds surging out of factories, or traffic at the Place de l'Opéra, or trains, or the leafy boughs over the heads of picnickers in the Bois de Boulogne."[41] It does so, furthermore, by developing in us a sensitivity to motion's "mysterious and complex grace" (Baudelaire's words). What is beyond the artistry of a painter or writer—depicting the "complex grace" of a carriage plowing through a muddy road or a ship precariously riding storm-tossed waves—is easily captured by the movie camera. Experiencing this special quality on film, which can be done again and again, builds up a new and expanded fascination for objects as such, whether static or moving.[42]

A deplorable failing in life is that we pay so little attention to what the senses offer. School teaches us how to use our mind but ignores the senses other than hearing and sight so that the world we learn to know in the classroom is essentially abstract and dead—fascinating, perhaps, but not lovable, and, if not lovable, then what motivation is there to care and protect it? School is not entirely to blame, for it has its hands full developing the mind.

Activating the senses, unlike activating the mind, does not require the same degree of tutoring. What is required is that we be reminded periodically of the powers at our disposal. Severe deprivation itself can be an effective reminder. After a heavy head cold, what glory spreads before us when the senses come to life again! All too soon, however, our gratitude and amazement pass, and we fall back to taking the sensorial riches of the environment for granted.

CHAPTER 13

What the Mind Can Offer

I HAVE DWELT ON THE SENSES, singing their praises to compensate for their neglect by the humanities. The senses may be a biological endowment, but it is the mind or culture that directs, expands, and intensifies their use. What, after all, is hearing without the glories of music or seeing without culture's directing us to the splendors of the stars and the moods of landscapes? I now turn more exclusively to the mind, beginning with language that is its singular feature and gives the mind its exceptional power.

LANGUAGE

What is language? What are its basic elements? As laymen our answer to the second and more specific question is likely to be "nouns," because we tend to see reality as made up of objects. Parents encourage young children to see reality this way when they point to objects and say to them, "This is a dog, and that is a mat; the dog sits on the mat." But isn't it plausible, asks C. S. Lewis, that what captures our attention is not the dog but a certain quality of doggyness? Lewis's own earliest experiences were of sheer quality. To him, "the terrible and the lovely are older and solider than terrible and lovely things." He then adds the insight, "If a musical phase could be translated into words at all it would become an adjective. A great lyric is very like a long, utterly adequate, adjective."[1]

Now consider place-names, the stuff that schoolchildren learn in geography class and find so boring. Place-names seem to be pure nouns, meaningless and difficult to remember, until they become adjectives, each capturing not only a distinctive quality of sight, sound, and smell, but also a distinctive historical association. Chinese place-names have more of the character of adjectives, which poets use to great effect, than do American ones. The latter are more like nouns little soaked in historical events and so seldom able to evoke a mood. Chinese place-names enjoy, in addition, a visual advantage. The ideograph that stands for a place can itself bolster the place's meaning in the thickness and firmness of its strokes and nodes.[2]

Words designate, but they also evoke a sense of something, and, when they do, they function as metaphors. Why isn't plain designation enough? Why can't words just have a literal meaning? The answer is that we are just not that sort of creature. We need to have a *feeling* for the objects around us, and one way to do so is to use words that are metaphorical. Topographical features, for example, are understandable and familiar to us—humanized—when we are able to link them to our own anatomy; and so we speak of the "spine" of a mountain, the "head" or "mouth" of a river, and an "arm" of the sea. Another challenge for us is to understand phenomena that are complex and ineffable. Metaphors come to the rescue in the form of simple, yet suggestive, images: God is a mighty fortress, a life is a river, and a man is either a wolf or a lamb.

Metaphors enrich life, making it more vivid. This is especially true when they are newly coined, but even much used ones retain a certain power. The "mouth" of a river, for example, is certainly not new. In fact, geographers don't even think of "mouth," used of a river, as figurative or poetical. Yet it does add an extra layer of meaning to the river's terminus and does so without misleading us as to its true nature. When the mother calls her child a lamb, something extra cuddly and innocent is added to the child, with no danger whatsoever of the mother mistaking her child's identity. On the other hand, metaphors can mislead. Consider the expression, "the mighty fortress is our God." While the metaphor helps us to latch on to one of God's attributes, it can through too frequent use make us forget His other attributes, which are infinite in number. Another example is the expression, "the brain is a computer," popular in cognitive science. The brain, an object of bewildering complexity, is simplified by the analogy, making it sufficiently comprehensible for scientists to probe into its workings, which they have done with considerable success. On the other hand, this particular figure of speech is approaching a point when it hinders rather than adds to further understanding.[3] Should scientists, then, give it up and try another figure? To go a step further, should science forbid all use of metaphor?

The thought already occurred to the Royal Society during the seventeenth century. Fortunately, it was not carried out. To give up metaphor altogether, even if it is possible, would be a grave error, for it is capable of initiating and guiding thought along fruitful lines. Ask the following questions: "Could Galileo (1564–1642) have arrived at his ideas of motion without the image of the galloping horse?" "How far could Charles Darwin (1809–1882) have gone with his theory of evolution without the master metaphor of a branching tree?" "Or Friedrich von Kekulé (1829–1896) with the structure of organic molecules without the image of a snake eating its own tail?" "Or Salvador Luria (1912–1991) with his study of bacterial mutation without seeing an analogy in the slot machine"?[4]

Metaphors that truly enrich or enlighten are the creations of a mature mind. Young children invent them in a spirit of fun; not surprisingly, they turn out to be largely nonsensical. As children grow older these are dropped in favor of ones that draw on perceptual similarity: for example, nuns are penguins, and batteries are rolled-up sleeping bags. Their next stage is to see a similarity that is psychological rather than perceptual: they understand, as they didn't when they were younger, such expressions as "you have a heart of stone" or comparing love to a summer's day. With each step a deeper understanding of human relations and human reality is achieved, even though, taken literally, the statements are clearly false.[5]

Now, what about stories? A good story is rich in metaphors, untrue in factual particulars yet true to human experience and condition. Stories are considered realistic when they have an abundance of down-to-Earth details that evoke real life. Many make no such attempt, and some are outright fantasies. All well-told stories—including and, perhaps, even especially fantasies—have the power to alter perception such that whatever is "out there" (reality) can never be quite the same again.

Consider Oxford, England. Tourists expect to see there a "sweet city" of "dreaming spires." Why "sweet city" and "dreaming spires" when modern Oxford has smelly factories and is largely an urban sprawl when seen from the air? Well, because Matthew Arnold (1822–1888) applied those words to the city, and what they evoke has become a fixture ever since.[6] Arnold is only one of many gifted writers who have written about Oxford or have used it as a setting for stories. The result is to enchant the city such that a well-read visitor who enters it finds himself immersed in the whimsical world of Lewis Carroll (1832–1898), the dandyish world of Max Beerbohm (1872–1956), and the snobbish world of Evelyn Waugh (1903–1966). He punts on the Cherwell and sees the Liddell girls absorbed in stories of Alice, walks on High Street and believes that he has caught a glimpse of Zuleika Dobson, strides across the Great Quad of Christ Church and can almost hear the drunken shouts of its aristocratic students, enters a paneled college room and expects to find Lord Peter Wimsey sipping sherry as he solves a murder case.

A few extraordinary stories have changed not just a city, but the world and not just for a time, but for the ages. Think of the great religious stories. How can they, with their lack of realism, have such power? "How" remains a mystery, but that they have the power is indisputable, since new civilizations have emerged in consequence of their telling.

Here are two familiar examples. The first, the life of Siddhartha Gautama—Buddha (560–480 BCE)—sounds like a fairy tale. It begins with a handsome prince living in a palace, which by all accounts is the perfect place, and yet the prince feels driven to abandon it and wander all over the continent in search of enlightenment. He eventually finds it while meditating under a tree. The second, the life of Jesus of Nazareth (c. 5 BCE–c. 30 CE), begins in a stable and ends on the cross, a more grim narrative compared with Buddha's—except, of course, for the resurrection. Does the resurrection make the story a fairy tale? Whatever the answer, the story of Jesus is undoubtably powerful and influential, and this is true not only of the authorized accounts, but also of accretions that scholars deem pure fabrication: for example, the story of the three kings who follow a star (a supernova?) to the birthplace of Jesus, bringing with them the gifts of gold, myrrh, and frankincense. To this day, even as materialism and worldliness gain ground, the tale of the three kings paying homage to a baby in a stable continues to stir something good in us. And this is not all. The sentiment continues to find expression in art, music, and literature, and these, in turn, have an impact on life.

Can a secular story have comparable impact? And does it also have to be simple such that it can be understood by ordinary men and women? The answer to both would seem to be "yes." For evidence I offer *Das Kapital: Kritik der Politischen Ökonomie* (1867), a large and complex work by Karl Marx (1818–1883) that is accessible only to scholars. Yet, when condensed into pamphlets and bolstered by lectures from academic and political pulpits, Marx's message does get through to the people. During the first half of the twentieth century, it succeeded in transforming much of the world's politics and life, ironically undercutting Marx's own belief that what matters are the material forces of production and not words and ideals, which are mere froth.

Transforming society into a Marxist/communist model turns out, however, to be short-lived, ending in 1989 with the fall of the Berlin Wall. Since then, the two giant communist states—Russia and China—have both abandoned *Das Kapital* as the guiding text. To the extent that Marx's narrative still exerts a sociopolitical influence, it is not so much from the dialectical materialist theory of change as from the belief that the poor have certain generative powers ("Blessed are the poor") that Marx borrowed from Christianity.

What about ordinary words—casual words? We experience their power every day. The casual remark, "Well, the service is rather slow," based on a single visit to a new restaurant, may be enough to steer friends away from it. And then there is the reputation of a colleague, so easy to tarnish with a phrase. To brighten it, however, would require greater verbal skill from us. The rule holds with words as with other efforts: namely, it is far easier to take down than to build up. Yet we can build up with good will and sensitivity. How? The Water Rat shows us how in *The Wind in the Willows* (1908), by Kenneth Grahame (1859–1932).

Mole and the Water Rat are good friends. Rat has entertained Mole in his rowing boat. Now it is Mole's turn to reciprocate the hospitality. But he is ashamed of his house, which he regards as a "poor, cold little place." Rat's generous response is to recreate his friend's house with words and gestures, "So compact! So well planned! Everything here and everything in its place!" He sets to build a fire, gets Mole to dust the furniture, but Mole discovers a new source of shame: there is no food.

"No bread!" groaned the Mole dolorously; "no butter, no—"

"No *pâté de fois gras*, no champagne!" continued the Rat, grinning. "Ah, that reminds me—what's that little door at the end of the passage? Your cellar of course. Every luxury in this house! Just you wait a minute."

Down Rat goes, and back he comes, a bottle of beer in each hand, and one under each arm. "Self-indulgent beggar you seem to be, Mole," he observed. "Deny yourself nothing. This is really the jolliest place I ever was in. Now wherever did you pick up those prints? Make the place so home-like, they do. No wonder you're fond of it, Mole. Tell us all about it and how you came to make it what it is."[6]

ARCHITECTURE

Birds build nests, and termites build skyscrapers, but animals don't have architecture in the sense of first forming an image—the image of an ideal—and then turning it into material reality. Humans do and for this reason they don't just build: they also have architecture. Architecture is capable of progress: successive envisagements (plans) lead to successive constructions.

Let me illustrate with the story of interior space. Knowing what it is like to be "inside" rather than "outside" is a human universal, yet the quality of that experience is radically different, depending on the sort of building one has access to. Begin with the ancient Egyptians of the third dynasty. They knew the sublimity of exterior space (think of the architect Imhotep's first pyramid at Saqqara in 2630 BCE under moonlight), but interior space for them was darkness and clutter. Ancient Greeks had the Parthenon (447–432 BCE) on top of the Acropolis to lift their spirit, but its interior was hardly more spacious than the interior of an Egyptian mortuary temple. Europeans had to wait for the construction of Hadrian's Pantheon (c. 126) to acquire, for the first time, the sense of an interior space that was formally elegant yet sublime—a vast hemisphere illuminated by the rotating sun.[7]

Another giant leap forward was the Gothic cathedral, which originated in twelfth–century France. Enter it, and one enters a hall of soaring pillars, fanning out at the ceiling like the branching foliage of a forest. Even more distinctive than the pointed arches and soaring pillars is the illumination. A Gothic cathedral is a vaulting space of shimmering lights and colors. It obtains these effects from the sunlight that pours through the stained-glass windows, from precious stones set in richly embroidered vestments, from gold-coated chalice and the bejeweled cross itself. To moderns, the colors cater to aesthetics: they make the interior more beautiful. But, to medievals, they also stood for Christian virtues—each color a virtue. Topping the visual splendor is the sobriety and splendor of music. The Gothic cathedral is a music box, filled in medieval times with subdued, rhythmic chants and, later, with the full sonority of Europe's greatest composers. In the right state of mind, the cathedral is a spiritual and multi-sensorial experience. No architectural space in the past offered a comparable richness of experience, and certainly none remotely do so now. No wonder the cathedral is called the forecourt of heaven.

Grandeur of exterior is much more readily achieved than grandeur of the interior. We have seen how the exterior soars and the interior constrains in Egyptian pyramids and mortuary temples and in Athens's Parthenon. Other examples are Tibet's Potala Palace (1645) and China's Temple of Heaven (1406–1420). The magnificent exterior of the Potala leads to small, dark rooms inside; the sweeping facade that produces in itself a feeling of spiritual elevation has to count on other symbolic means—flickering oil lamp, statues, and monks prostrate in prayer—to sustain the spiritual message. As for the interior of the Temple of Heaven, its elaborate ceiling of wooden beams rising to a peak does invite the upward glance but without the sensation of soaring that is a common experience of entering a Gothic cathedral. Chinese architects, even if they wished, didn't have the technical means to create a light-filled space of great size that can give the illusion of floating. In traditional Chinese architecture, the nearest to a sublime interior is the great courtyard, closed to the profane world but open to the sky.

Modern architects would seem to have all the technics they need to fulfill their dreams. The result, somewhat surprisingly, is a return to exterior magnificence. Buildings such as the Guggenheim Museum in Bilbao (1997), by Frank Gehry (b. 1949), and the Central Television Tower Beijing (2009), by Rem Koolhaas (b. 1949), are monumental sculptures that cater to the eye. The eye, let us remember, is not only tolerant of novelty, but may insist on it. By contrast, the body as a whole is conservative, its comfort zone narrow. The architect cannot create interior spaces that flow into each other or surfaces that curve, bend, and tilt without causing disorientation to the point of dizziness and nausea. At best, these geometries draw attention to themselves, distracting not only visitors from appreciating the paintings in a museum, as can happen in the Guggenheim Museum in New York City (1959), by Frank Lloyd Wright (1867–1959), but also office workers from concentrating on the businesses at hand, as might happen in Koolhass's Tower.

No such cross-purpose occurs in religious architecture. The worshiper, upon entering a cathedral, mosque, or temple, is supposed to think of God. Prayers, hymns, chants, the reading of lessons, and the sermon all direct attention to the One. Far from being supernumerary, architecture is central to the total spiritual experience. In a curious way, the showpiece buildings of our time are a return to the showpiece buildings of antiquity in that both counterpose a splendid exterior against a modest interior. They do so, however, for very different reasons. Ancient builders lacked the technology to construct a spacious and spiritually elevating interior. Modern builders have no need of it. In our secular age, the closest to a "spiritual" experience is when we enter a museum to look at its paintings or a concert to listen to a symphony. All too often the interior we enter is a busy hotel lobby or the hushed offices and corridors of the corporate world. Whatever the reason, we certainly don't enter to meet God! So where is the inspiration—the ultimate inspiration—for the architect?

Spaciousness is an experience that nature offers us in abundance. So one would think, yet even here architecture plays a guiding role. Consider Jeffrey Tate's experience at Amiens Cathedral (1220–1270) along the River Somme in France. Tate (b. 1943) suffered a spinal defect in childhood that hobbled him, making his life as the conductor of the Royal Opera difficult. Even walking was a struggle. He told a friend that, when he entered the cathedral, he had the most extraordinary sensation of space opening up before him. He felt he could float.[8] Amiens Cathedral is known for its size and height, but do we really need architecture for a prehension of size? After all, even St. Peter's basilica is small compared with the valley in which it is located. Yet not the valley but the building gives us a sense of commanding size and height. The building has this power by virtue of its clearly articulated proportions, which direct and educate our sight lines. Nature seldom has such geometric clarity, and, when it does, we describe it as sculptural or architectural.

Two more examples reveal how our sense of space is extended by cultural-technological means. Begin with the question, "What gives us the most basic notion of space?" Answer: not sight—the eye's ability to see objects disposed three-dimensionally "out there"—but rather our ability to move. An infant kicks its legs—that's the start. Reaching out the arm opens up more space. Throwing a stone and seeing it fly through the air opens up still more. And so on. The spaces continue to expand as techniques of ejection improve from throwing a spear with the strength of the arm to throwing it with the added power of a spear-thrower, from shooting an arrow with a taut bow to firing a bullet and, eventually, to sending rocket and spacecraft into the blue yonder. As technology gives us more power, what begins as a kinesthetic experience (throwing a stone) turns into visual perception (the arrow flying into the air) and, eventually, into an abstract understanding of spatial extent. In other words, space as *felt* diminishes. Whether an abstract understanding can also give one a feeling of vastness is for the mathematically talented to answer.

The second example is when we ourselves move through space. The swifter we move—from crawling to walking, to running—the more space opens out and becomes less a barrier to surmount than a lure to freedom. With the domestication of the horse, humans experienced a different order of swiftness. Imagine the riders' sense of freedom as they raced their horses across the Mongolian steppe! Machines likewise liberate. Think of the successive gains in speed and maneuverability in such machines as the bicycle, motorbike, sports car, and light-weight airplane that can soar and dive like a swallow. Ironically, as the machine gets bigger, more powerful, and speedier, the feel for space and spaciousness begins to diminish. Passengers strapped in the cushy seats of a jumbo airplane have the immobility of babies, their space and feeling for space reduced to a minimum. Astronauts, far from enjoying spatial immensity, know foremost only the confined space of their spacecraft; far from feeling the power of motion in themselves, they are aware only of their own weightlessness, floating with no ability to accelerate or decelerate on their own volition in a spacecraft that itself seems motionless, an object suspended in the pitch-black sky.

Space is intimately linked to time in ordinary life, as we shall see later. But here I will mention one such link, because it derives from speed of motion that I have just noted and because it is a link that is widely known only in the last twenty years or so. Here is what I have in mind. The speed of news transmission and the speed of our own mobility have, together, significantly extended our sense of the present by shortening what we consider to be the past. Not so long ago, no news from a distant place is never contemporary: whatever one hears is of the past. People live in the present but are surrounded by pastness all around them. Today, even news that comes to me from the other side of Earth is current. I am surrounded by presentness, the past being wiped out by the speed of communication. What if *I* do the moving rather than the news? Then, again, the present expands and the past contracts. In 1941, it took me three weeks to go by boat from Hong Kong to Sydney. Returning to Hong Kong, I could write off the Australian city as my past, for it is unlikely that I would ever have the time to cross all that space again. I can now cross it in twelve hours. The result is that Sydney is almost as much my present as Hong Kong. The two cities are becoming the two ends of a circular route—a commute! And all commutes are experienced as occurring in an extended present.

The speed of travel and, even more, the speed of electronic communication have radically diminished space. For the practical purposes of life, such as the conduct of business, space is a barrier, and so we may want it diminished. In other situations and experiences, however, space continues to be life-enhancing and remains a potent metaphor for something good. Thus, we may say of a great work of art that it gives us a sense of space, as though we have been invited into "some large hall of reflection" and of friendship that it is one in which each provides the other with resonant space.[9] "Friendship," says Roland Barthes, "may be defined as a space with total sonority."[10]

TIME

The senses give us the world, but they don't give us a major dimension of that world: time. We may speak loosely of a "sense of time," but there is no such sensory organ. Time is something we experience and construct. Time is experienced—is felt—when we wait, expect, or hope. Waiting can be serene, as when I wait in a contemplative mood for illumination. Mostly, however, it is stressful, for it reduces me to passivity. Expectation, if it is of something good in the future, is a positive feeling, yet it can also be felt as passivity: this happens when that which is expected comes to us. Expectation that doesn't anchor me in place—waiting—but rather motivates me to move forward to the desired object is indistinguishable from hope. Hope sees the future as prospect, toward which I move.

Time may also be experienced as rhythms of the body: breathing in and out; the alternation of sleep and wakefulness, of energy and fatigue; and as rhythmic motions of the body, the arms and legs swinging back and forth as one walks. The painfulness of waiting (empty time) is alleviated by rhythmic time, such as drumming fingers, rocking back and forth in an armchair, or pacing. Time is experienced directionally in the entropy of energy—one feels increasingly tired toward the end of the day and increasingly feeble in the twilight years of life. Travel is another source of directionality: the "here" and "there"of space aligned with the "now" and "then" of time.

Time felt in the body as swinging and cyclical motions is confirmed by parallels in nature: for example, the back-and-forth motion of the waves on the seashore and of the tide in an estuary, the sun's arc from morning to night, and changing seasons from winter through spring to summer and then back again to autumn and winter. Neither the swing nor the cycle is directional taken as a whole: but if one attends to just one part of the swing—for example, either the rise or the retreat of the tide—it has the feel of directionality. For time as pure directionality, the river is undoubtedly a less ambiguous image.

Although these experiences of time are common, they are not consciously recognized unless the environment or the culture or both draw attention to them. Take a tropical rainforest. The hunter-gatherers who live in it breathe in-and-out as all animals and humans do, and like all humans they swing their arms as they walk; but there is no reason for them to consider these biological rhythms as types of temporal measure. Time is not on their mind nor, for that matter, is it on ours as we go through the average day. Will the hunter-gatherers notice pendulum-like or cyclical changes in their environment? No. In equatorial latitudes, the diurnal cycle is too unvarying and the seasonal cycle too faint to command attention. Plants and animals in the rainforest do change; they have stages of maturation that, when recognized, can suggest directional or cyclical time. But the stages may not be recognized. The Mbuti of northeastern Congo, for instance, know much about the flora and fauna upon which they depend yet reveal surprising lacunae: they do not grasp that the aquatic larvae they eat turn into mosquitoes or that the caterpillar turns into butterfly.[11] Besides the absence of seasons, the absence of distance contributes to the Mbuti's incognizance of time's passage. In the dense forest, the hunter-gatherers are always close to what they see or need. The animal they hunt, when they see it, is right in front of them. They have no notion of a desirable object or goal that will take them effort and time to reach. There is no "here" and "there" sufficiently far apart and requiring effort to overcome that demand to be noticed and translated into the temporal terms of "now" and "then."

In sharp contrast to the rainforest is the desert. Australian aborigines, who are also hunter-gatherers and whose level of material culture is comparable to that of the Mbuti, live in the great open spaces, where they can see far and need to see far to orient themselves and be aware of the possible locations of water and food. Unlike the Mbuti who, in their rich environment, can find sustenance everywhere, Australian aborigines must be on the move in search of it. Their life is a journey on paths trodden and created by their ancestors. For people on the move there is always the "here" of where they now stand and the "there" of their next stop. It takes time to make the journey, time measured by the expenditure of effort and by changes in scenery, time that is directional as the journey is directional. Australian aborigines cannot help being aware of directional time for another reason: the importance to them of narrating the mythic journeys of their ancestors as a part of their ritual life. These narrations are structured events that occur in temporal sequence.[12]

To go from these simple cultures to Western civilization is a leap yet is justified by shared experiences that underlie people's basic notions of time. Western civilization is rooted in ancient Israel and Greece. The Israelites or Hebrews had a reputation for being frequently on the move; the word "Hebrew" itself meant "donkey-man, caravaneer, or dusty," a man whose donkey raised dust on a much-traveled road. An event of foremost importance to the Hebrews was the great migration called Exodus. Moses led his people out of bondage in Egypt (c. 1300 BCE) to the edge of Canaan, a journey of forty years over harsh deserts during which the people suffered much and yet remained faithful to God. Canaan—the Promised Land—already had occupants, an agricultural people who, in the eyes of the Hebrews, indulged their senses, loved wealth, and worshiped place-bound deities called Baalim. Time, for them, would have been cyclical, like that of all those who worked on the land, their schedule of activities geared to the motions of the sun. The Hebrews, with their nomadic background and a taste for austerity recently enforced by wanderings in the wilderness, took for granted they had the right to displace the adulators of Baalim, settle themselves there, and live under the God of history—which is to say, God of sequential time that has a beginning, a middle, and a culminating end.

The worldview of the other root of Western civilization—Greek—was spatial and place-centered, focusing, at one end of the scale, on cosmic space and, at the other end of the scale, on place or locality. Cosmic space gave the Greeks, insofar as they were farmers, a cyclical notion of time. The elite, however, also had a linear sense of time, based on their pride of ancestry. Citizens of rival cities claimed that they and they alone had descended from a long line of ancestors, the naming of whom—one after another—gave them a sense of time as succession. Unlike the Hebrews, who also boasted about their lineage, the Greeks lacked a master narrative that was sequential—what we now call "history"—for they didn't have a God who strode through time, causing or supervising events such that they never went irredeemably off course. Another major difference between Hebrews and Greeks was this: unlike the Hebrews, the Greeks—outstandingly Plato (429–347 BCE)—embraced an idea—eternity—that transcended time altogether.

Christianized Europe adopted Judaism's God of history and, with it, a story line that has a beginning, a middle, and an end—a story leading to salvation. But once Christianity became the established religion of settled peoples, it also embraced a cosmic and cyclical notion of time, manifest in a calendar of seasonal rituals that resembled those of pagan, natural religions. To be a Christian was and is to live in both senses of time, to be engaged with place and the routine of this world, which means experiencing time as cyclical, and to be a pilgrim on the path to salvation, which means experiencing time as linear and directional. In the Catholic Church, most rituals—their Christian roots notwithstanding—follow nature's cycles, an exception being the Stations of the Cross, in which pilgrims retrace successive incidents in the Passion of Christ; that is, they follow a directional path. Compared with the Catholic church, Protestant churches give more importance to sermons, and sermons are stories that have direction and a point, like the story of Christ's life. As for eternity, it lingered on in Christian thought, as did Platonic ideas generally, through the millennia. Serious engagement with it was and is, however, largely confined to philosophical theologians and mystics.

Outside the church and its rites, cyclical and linear conceptions of time have changed with shifting conditions in the world: now the one, now the other comes to the fore. In Europe, the art of painting tells the story of one such change. Prior to the rise of landscape as a subject around 1400, European paintings—most of which had a religious theme—may have featured the cross or the saint in the foreground, a background of little depth, and possibly a gold disk at the top that represented the sun. A composition that is essentially flat, with the sun placed at the zenith, is compatible with a cyclical conception of time. Eventually, the sun lowers to the horizon, and the viewer's eyes are drawn to it or to some other eye-catching feature, such as a patch of blue sky or a church steeple, across an expanse of space. In landscape painting, both space and time acquire direction. Both flow outward from where the viewer stands to the distant horizon, from the "here"' that is "now" to the "there" that is "then."[13]

What if, at the horizon and even beyond it, lay not the setting sun, patch of blue sky, or church steeple but paradise—the New World? The rise of landscape painting as a prestigious art form was quickly followed by the age of great explorations. As landscape artists no longer looked upward for paradise but outward to a distant point on the horizon, so did the explorers, though their sight was always earthbound. This ninety-degree shift from cosmos to landscape marked the end of the medieval frame of mind and the beginning of the early modern, the change being from religious to secular, from a goal in heaven to a goal in geographical space.[14]

Directional time implies progress. The idea of progress has roots in antiquity when advancements in technology first became evident. Its upsurge since 1500 was not, however, solely the result of an awareness that better and more powerful instruments and machines were being built. It also received encouragement from the artists' success in achieving what they believed to be the perfect representation of a landscape. That achievement depended on both the invention of new mechanical devices, such as the camera obscura, and on the ever more skilled use of perspectival geometry.[15] By 1800, artists began to feel they had gone as far as they could go. Evidence of progress turned to accomplishments in other areas and, by the nineteenth century, to the area of actual landscape transformation. Historians, geographers, and the conservation-minded could see that far more than the small steps in the perfection of landscape art, or even the larger steps of technological innovation, were the huge steps of turning forests into farms, farms into villages and towns and thence into cities and megalopolises, which may well be characterized as forests of soaring glass-and-steel.

A reaction against progress and, consequently, also against a linear conception of time emerged forcefully toward the end of the nineteenth century. It was argued that progress occurred not only at the expense of nature, but also of humans who happened to be in the way. Moreover, constant and even accelerated advancement was not sustainable. At some point in the future the natural systems that sustain life could collapse. And so another line of thinking found favor, elaborated under the auspices of biology rather than of the physical and mechanical sciences. It came to be known as ecology.[16] A fundamental principle of ecology is interdependence: whatever happens in one part of a biotic system affects, sooner or later, all other parts. The cycle rather than the arrow, a circular rather than a linear conception of time, and interdependence rather than lineal causality are the dominant realities. Nevertheless, that other major innovation in biology—evolution—had to be accommodated with ecology's more static view. The result is that any sweeping account of life on Earth has to reconcile two conceptions of time: cyclical and linear. Moreover, the biologist's caveats notwithstanding, to most people "linear" and "directional" imply progress.

Time as direction raises the question, "How long and how far?" To hunter-gatherers the arrow of time is very short. Their sense of the past turns fuzzy beyond their grandparents, and, since they have no strong sense of the future either, they live pretty much in the present. By contrast the past in hierarchical societies may reach back several generations. The desire for prestige encourages one to boast a long lineage—the longer and more distinguished, the better. As I noted earlier, both the Greeks and Hebrews so boasted. Even today, lineage matters. Americans see their standing in society as the reward of their own accomplishments, yet ancestry still counts and prestige accrues to those who can trace their descent from passengers of the *Mayflower*.

Our sense of directional time is asymmetrical: whereas projection into the past is helped by names and material markers, projection into the future has no such support and, therefore, quickly runs into vagueness. Politicians are fond of saying, "We must do this for the sake of our children and our children's children." Sounds good and farsighted. The words have a grave, biblical rhythm to them, but what politicians really want is to have their pet projects approved and credited to them now. I doubt they can envisage their grandchildren's future in any detail as either starving on thin gruel or as living high on the hog. This becomes clear to me when, taking my cue from God's promise to Abraham, I greet a student-father with the words, "Congratulations! You are on your way to being a founder of nations!" He is astonished. He has never given a thought to that distant prospect, far less the likelihood that, a thousand years hence, among the numerous descendants of his newborn child there may be an Archimedes (c. 287–c. 212 BCE)—or a Hitler (1889–1945).

Civilizations differ in their knowledge of temporal duration. China, even though it prides itself on the keeping of historical records and even though it constantly refers to a Golden Age in the past, has a shallow sense of time. A reason might be its worldview, which assumes a cosmos that has always existed and that, therefore, lacks a story line. Another might be that, since Chinese buildings are made mostly of timber, which is liable to decay and easily destroyed by fire, its landscape lacks architectural markers of time. In this respect, China differs strikingly from Europe, which has many such markers, going all the way back to the prehistoric Stonehenge (c. 2500 BCE). Yet Europe, despite such markers and a worldview that includes an act of creation, had a shallow sense of time until well into the eighteenth century; and, even then, such was the baneful influence of the *Bible* that a learned man such as Samuel Johnson (1709–1784) could bandy about the figure 4004 BCE as the year of Earth's probable birth. He was, however, out of touch with the advanced thinking of his time. A new science of geology emerged that vastly expanded the age of Earth. Johnson's contemporary, James Hutton (1726–1797), studied the stratigraphic record and could see in it "no vestige of a beginning and no prospect of an end."[17]

Among civilizations India is exceptional in its conception of temporal vastness. Buddhists speak of *kalpas*, each of which lasts 1,280,000,000 years. As though this number may still fail to impress, they use similes to invoke time's immensity. Here is an example: "Suppose there is a mountain, of a very hard rock, much bigger than the Himalayas; and suppose that a man, with a piece of cloth once every century should touch that mountain ever so lightly—then the time which it would take for him to wear away the entire mountain would be about the temporal span of a *kalpa*."[18]

Standing at the edge of expansive space makes us dizzy, but standing at the edge of expansive time has no such effect. For all the persuasiveness of Indian metaphysicians and for all the hard data of geological time supplied by Western scientists, time's unbounded reach simply doesn't sink into our consciousness and psyche. At least rarely. But it can happen, as it did me when I lived in Albuquerque, New Mexico. About 100 miles west of Albuquerque on the Ramah Navajo Indian Reservation is the El Moro National Monument (established in 1906), the principal attraction of which are Pueblo ruins, pre-Columbian petroglyphs, and hundreds of signatures carved by travelers in the soft sandstone monolith rising more than 200 feet above the valley floor. The inscriptions date back to the seventeenth century, when Spanish explorers passed that way. They are now protected by glass plates. When I visited the monument in

1962, only a few tourists paid much attention to the signatures; most strolled about or prepared food for picnicking, and children frolicked and sent their thrill voices into the desert air. I was alone. I looked at the signatures. They were at first only mildly interesting, and then, quite unexpectedly, they plunged me into the abyss of time. What struck me was a thought: in 300 years, the cliff face has not retreated enough to remove the signatures, yet I knew from geology books that its original position could be a-half mile away. Three centuries of human history are a respectable length, but 500,000 years, the time for rain wash and wind to cause the cliff to retreat by a-half mile, is a mere blink in Earth's history. After this experience I thought I can never again enjoy a mountain view, since whatever spatial exhilaration it offers will be canceled by the monstrous chasm of time. Needless to say, this hasn't happened. I still enjoy the mountain scene. Forgetfulness and just plain dullness of imagination keep me and my fellow humans sane.

Geological strata register time. So do buildings. Indeed, the cultural historian and humanist Lewis Mumford (1895–1990) saw the city as time made visible. Not all cities, obviously. Many American cities look as though they have sprouted overnight. The traditional Chinese city is a cosmic diagram and, as such, timeless. The buildings in a Chinese city are not good time-markers either. Their original date of construction may be old, but they may well have been rebuilt several times since. What is retained is form rather than substance. Moreover, unless one is an architectural expert, even the form doesn't register time clearly, for changes in Chinese architectural style, such as in roof curvature, are not eye-catching, unlike the striking stylistic innovations in European architecture from Romanesque to Gothic, to Baroque, to nineteenth-century eclecticism, to Modernism and post-Modernism. So it is principally the old European city that is time made visible, thanks not only to buildings of different ages and styles, but also, in some cities, to the successive rings of urban expansion. Paris is an outstanding example of the latter. From the old core on an island in the River Seine the city grew so that successive walls—those of the thirteenth century, the seventeenth century, and the period between 1789 and 1840—had to be built to protect the inhabitants. The walls were eventually torn down and replaced by ring roads. As I look at the ring roads on a map, I can't help thinking of tree rings.[19]

Americans, though fixated on the future, were and are remarkably sentimental about the past. Cities of any size and pride are expected to have a museum. Even nineteenth-century frontier towns might have had a store that also served as a museum, displaying antiquated machinery, furniture, and old maps and photos.[20] Therefore, it is surprising to know that neither China and India—the old Asian civilizations—nor Europe had museums until the eighteenth century. In Europe, museums began as private collections of curiosities, and the emphasis was initially on "curiosity" rather than on age or artistic merit. Even now, how aware are we of time when we visit the museum? Aren't we still inclined to see the displays as curiosities or, if we are learned, as documents of the past from which we can derive present knowledge? Few of us can say, as John Updike says: "It frightens him, as museums used to frighten him, when it was part of school to take trips there and see the mummy rotting in his casket of gold, the elephant tusk filed into a hundred squinting Chinamen. Unthinkably distant lives, abysses of existence, worse than what crawls blind on ocean floors."[21]

The existence of "museums" in American frontier towns did not mean that the residents sought to hold on to their roots or believed that their identity lay in the past. To the contrary, their orientation was very much to the future. The odd pieces of old furniture and farming tools were, if anything, reminders to them of how far they had progressed. The old bedstead and plow might have been used by their parents only a few decades ago and yet already had slipped far enough into the past to seem curiosities. Quite different from such attitude was the one that emerged during the second half of the twentieth century. Americans, feeling ever more rootless in a rapidly changing social and technological landscape, actively sought reassurance in ancestral roots. Genealogy became a popular hobby, and towns with any ethnic flavor strove to enhance it by resurrecting old buildings and customs and organizing festivals and performances that drew attention to them. In part, this was a response to economic necessity. As manufacturing declined there grew an increasing need to find other sources of income—and one of the most promising was tourism; for lack of grain, timber, or tractors to sell, one could always offer one's dolled-up grandma. But this is not to deny that there did exist among townspeople a genuine desire to recover the simpler and more culturally distinct ways of their forebears. What they desired to recover was, needless to say, highly selective, choosing the pleasing and fair against the ugly and harsh.[22]

I began my discussion of time with the personal and the universal—the uneasy time of waiting and expectation and the bright time of hope—and moved from there to different cultural conceptions of time. These cultural conceptions of time, however, rarely affected the feelings and moods of individuals. As I have noted, even though I knew the age of Earth from textbooks, time remained a numerical abstraction and not something I could feel—a threatening abyss—until my visit to the El Moro National Monument. So what are the occasions when time is felt personally?

"*J'ai failli attendre*," Louis XIV exclaimed, as he walked into the audience chamber. He stepped in barely a minute after his courtier had made his entry. The shock was that he, the Sun King, almost had to wait. There is no clearer indicator of status than who waits for whom. Time rather than space is definitive, for time is life, and even the most powerful have only a limited number of years to live. In the end, it is a question of whose time—that is to say, whose life—is more valuable. The soldier invariably waits for his sergeant, the cab driver for his fare, the lover for his beloved. Inequality of power and standing, which exists in all societies, makes suffering the languid flow of time a fact of life for everyone. What we tend to forget is that people have also had to wait for nature's pleasure. Farmers all over the world know what it is like to scan the sky, day after cloudless day, for a sign of rain.

Life in a modern, affluent society is more confident. The future is inviting, rather like virgin territory to be colonized. We march into it with assured steps until we stumble over an unexpected obstacle, a setback during which time grinds to a stop and the future seems like a wall. But the obstacle is overcome, and time opens out again to accommodate our next project. And so life goes on, hopeful yet tinged with anxiety. One anxiety is, however, of another order and implacable, deeply buried in our consciousness and not really allowed to surface until it does as chest pain at three o'clock in the morning. I refer to anxiety about death—its possibility at any moment and without warning. In bright moods, time may be to us a sun-dappled landscape, but, in darker moods, we know that its potholes and ditches can break our stride—and our neck.

Time passes inexorably whether we will or not. One way to gain a sense of control over it is to divide it into parts—morning, noon, afternoon, and evening; dawn, day, dusk, and night; the four phases of the moon; the four seasons. All people periodize time in some such fashion. Another way, developed furthest in the Western world, is to measure time with an instrument of our own device. We in the West feel that the more accurately we can measure time, the more we are in control of it and so make it serve our ends. Sundial, hourglass, clock, and watch are timepieces of increasing precision. In the ordinary businesses of life, however, the opposite often turns out to be the case: far from providing a feeling of control the clock and the watch habituate us to a time-consciousness so acute and demanding that we feel enslaved. But there is a third way, which does give us a sense of control. It occurs when time is made to submit to moral dictates. One such dictate is the promise. To promise is to bind a future, limiting its opennness and uncertainty. Another dictate, uniquely developed in the Christian West, is forgiveness. To forgive is to erase a past, depriving it of its power to stain the present.

IMAGINATION AND FANTASY

Imagination and fantasy are the stuff of everyday life, a consequence of our possessing a mind. Human senses, as I noted earlier, are powerful and subtle because they are backed by it. The mind's product—culture—in turn affects the senses, action, and mental processes. Powers so commonplace are yet held suspect by educated people of an empirical bent. When friends say that I am imaginative, I take it to be a compliment, provided it is not repeated. Repeated, and I conclude that they hold me to be out of touch with reality. To be called a fanciful person, or a person who likes fantasy, is even more dismissive. Clearly realism, being in touch with the real and grounded in common sense, is the desideratum. But why should this be so? All animals are, after all, grounded in common sense and in touch with the real. We humans have survived, which can only mean that we, too, for all our inclination to fantasize, are no different. What nevertheless distinguishes us from other animals is this: more than adapt to what exists—an ecology, an environment—we make a conscious effort to picture something better and then try to give the envisaged material form. Insofar as we succeed in making the change, we owe it to our imagination and our command of the facts.

Imagination and command of the facts are distinct qualities. Some people are better endowed in the one than the other; some people value one more than the other. Consider a few of these human types, starting with scientists. They are realists, enamored of empirical data and suspicious of fantasy. So we believe, yet some great scientists do not fit this description. Albert Einstein (1829–1955), for example, is reported to have said that, when examining his methods of thought, the gift of fantasy meant more to him than his talent for collecting facts.[23] In a way, we nonscientists are not too surprised, for, to us, Einstein's ideas about relativity and space-time continuum, no matter how true, are the very stuff of fantasy. A radical difference, then, separates ordinary people's fantasizing, which is little more than daydreaming and wishful thinking, and that of a scientist. The scientist's fantasy is the opposite of escapist self-indulgence; rather, it is a disciplined flight of the mind at the end of which reality is revealed to have unsuspected strangeness and beauty. What are the pre-conditions for such flight? They are exceptional curiosity, a temperament that favors the simple, a spirit of fun, and a keen appreciation of beauty.

Let me give an example of each. First, exceptional curiosity. Physicist Hans Bethe (1902–2005), when he was five years old, said to his mother while they were taking a walk, "Isn't it strange that if a zero comes at the end of the number it means a lot, but if it is at the beginning of a number it doesn't mean anything at all?"[24] At age five I could do simple sums by following the rules. Even a talented chimpanzee can do as much. Neither of us, however, will find the position of zero worth puzzling over. Our level of curiosity just doesn't reach that level.

Second, simplicity. Temperamentally, I appreciate complexity and richness in human work. I can enjoy a beautiful and ornate church service, for example. Not so, apparently, Galileo. When he was compelled to attend church, he filtered out all the ritual and spectacle in order to concentrate on one of the sacred lamps that swung back and forth on its chain. He pondered over the forces at work and decided that the motion depended on the length of the chain and on Earth's force of gravity. He was able to express the relationship in a mathematical equation that gave physics students much pleasure in his time and in the succeeding centuries. At a practical level, Galileo's formulation made accurate clocks possible.

Third, a spirit of fun, a delight in games. As a child I lacked both. I knew of children who liked nothing better than to make up rules and see where they led, if logically and systematically pursued. Some of the greatest discoveries in mathematics and science are the result of this sort of game playing. Take the example of Giovanni Girolamo Sacchari (1667–1733). In 1733, as an intellectual sport he submitted Euclid's axiom of parallels with the "nonsensical" axiom that, through a given point, two lines may be drawn parallel to a given line. From this start he constructed a self-consistent, non-Euclidean geometry. And that was that so far as Sacchari was concerned. He didn't realize that he had made a great discovery, one that led to a whole constellation of contrasting geometries, including the Riemannian, which Einstein was able to use as the mathematical key in the release of atomic energy.[25]

Fourth, a keen appreciation of beauty. A curious whim of the modern art world is, for many, to shun the word "beauty." It is not often used in praise. For most artists, "beauty" has come to mean or represent the bland and the trivial. The preferred encomium is "powerful" and even "ugly but powerful."[26] Banished by so many artists, "beauty" as a word of approval is now firmly installed among scientists; it is their favorite word of praise. Does this seem surprising? It shouldn't, for what are scientists after? They are after some sort of harmony in the chaos that is nature; and, obviously, the simpler and more elegant the harmony they find, the better they are pleased and the more likely they are to call their finding "beautiful." An unsuccessful theory is cumbersome and likely to be so full of arbitrary parameters that it threatens to approximate nature's own chaos. Such a theory, it goes without saying, is not only useless, but ugly.

Beauty by itself is, however, empty—a froth—unless it bespeaks truth. So scientific thinkers, from Pythagoras (c. 570–490 BCE) to Bertrand Russell, believed. What mystified them was that something so abstract and elegant as a mathematical equation could precisely express regularities (laws) in the seemingly messy physical world. The most recent scientist to confess his bewilderment and wonder is Subrahmanyan Chandrasekhar (1910–1995), the Nobel Laureate in physics who wrote: "In my entire scientific life, extending over forty-five years, the most shattering experience has been the realization that an exact solution of Einstein's equations of general relativity, discovered by the New Zealand mathematician, Roy Kerr, provides the absolutely exact representation of untold numbers of massive black holes that populate the universe. This 'shuddering before the beautiful,' this incredible fact that a discovery motivated by the search after the beautiful in mathematics should find its exact replica in Nature, persuades me to say that beauty is that to which the human mind responds at its deepest and most profound."[27]

The words "inevitable" and "exact" are laudatory in science. What about the arts? Since the arts make no general claim to being accurate representations of reality and since in the arts fantasy is allowed and even encouraged, the words would seem inapplicable. And yet, strange to say, it is in music—the most abstract and fanciful of the arts—that they do not seem out of place. When one listens to J. S. Bach's *Suite No. 6 for cello* (1723), Mozart's *Ave verum corpus in D minor* (1791), or any of their other supreme works of that era, one feels that they carry immense authority—the authority of the inevitable—of something beyond human ingenuity and will. If one is made to listen to music one does not particularly like, however, it is tempting to dismiss it as technically clever, even original, but original in the sense of being willfully different rather than in the sense of uncovering a treasure from the musical chest of heaven. But this response to supreme music as inevitable and exact—exact in that not a single note is superfluous or missing—can only be an illusion. Beethoven has made that clear in his treatment of his *String quartet in B flat*, opus 130 (1825). It ends with an uncompromisingly difficult, dissonant fugal finale—the Gross Fugue. When critics objected, Beethoven obligingly substituted an amiable movement that stood somewhere between Hayden and Schubert. Imagine a physicist so altering his theory of a mathematical proof!

Let us now turn to the art form called fiction and to fiction writers. Note, first, how we treat children differently, depending on whether their gift is in mathematics or in storytelling. We regard a child who wonders why the position of zero, whether it comes before or after a numeral, matters so much as showing real talent in mathematics or physics. Such fanciful thinking, we say, is good and should be encouraged. When, however, a child talks to an imaginary friend or tells himself a tall story, our reaction is less approving. At best we smile and say that he will outgrow this stage and come down to Earth. Why the difference? I suppose the answer is that, in the one case, imagining and fantasizing can lead eventually to truths about physical reality; in the other, they lead to what? A career in fiction writing? Even a successful career in fiction writing is still dismissable as producing mere entertainments, unless it offers truths about who we are and the sort of world we live in.

Realistic fiction claims to do just that. The characters may all be invented, but they plausibly exist, as does the world they live in. What, then, about works that are frankly fantasies, far removed from everyday life, such as myths, fairy tales, and science fiction? The good ones have several claims on our attention. One *is* entertainment, and why not? Surely, brief breaks from the swarming challenges and dull routines of life are allowable. More seriously, fantasies deserve our respect because they have their own internal logic, one that has to be all the more rigorous since their *mises-en-scène* of magic wands and fire-breathing dragons challenge belief. Fantasies are, in this sense, rather like mathematical theorems, to be valued for their internal coherence and beauty. Moreover, just as pure mathematics—the weaving of abstract patterns—can throw light on physical nature, revealing hitherto unsuspected dimensions, so might fantasies, by virtue of their simplicity, throw light on the murky depths and bright heights of human existence and give us a glimpse of, say, heaven and hell. Lastly, fantasies play a significant role in our moral life: they can change our attitude and behavior for the better, if only by little.[28]

REALITY, FANTASY, AND MORALITY

The last claim for fantasy is somewhat surprising, so let me elaborate. Rival literary genres, such as philosophy, history, and journalism, may surfeit us with ideas and facts, tell us about the dilemmas of human existence, and provide subtle pictures of good and evil, but they do not and are not intended to make us into better human beings. Realist fiction, by contrast, is more likely to have some such effect, even against the author's intention. It can do so for two reasons: one, it reveals people's inner feelings and thoughts that are the basis of moral stocktaking, and, two, it pays attention to the prosaic—and the prosaic world is one in which we mostly live. Both strengths, common in fiction, are rare in works of philosophy, history, and journalism.

Consider a great work of fiction, *Anna Karenina* (1877), by Leo Tolstoy (1828–1910). A famous scene shows Anna in a train, on her way to St. Petersburg and thinking fondly of her seven-year-old son. She can hardly wait to see him, but, when they finally meet, she is surprised by a fleeting sensation of disappointment. Somehow the boy doesn't quite measure up to her image of him. Now, although that feeling is not unusual, Tolstoy's reminding us of it makes us a little ill at ease, perhaps because it forces us to acknowledge ambiguity in even the most loving relationship. We may learn from the awareness and become a little more sensitive, but we can hardly expect to be better people as a result. Tolstoy is also accomplished in prosaics. He can make even the most commonplace of events seem important. An example is Natasha's happily showing off her baby's stained diaper at the end of *War and Peace* (1869). That image just might implant a usable moral lesson, which is that we heed the basics—and the prosaics—of life even against the immense and horrendous backdrop of war.

Tolstoy, in his old age, belittled his two long novels. What the world regarded as masterpieces he came to regard as little more than entertainments for the rich with time on their hands. They reminded him, in scale and pretension, of the grand operas that he attended as a young man but grew to dislike. Favored by him were his short stories and fables, which could be read and understood by people with modest education and which have a clear moral message. And so I return to the opinion I gave earlier, which is that fables and fairy tales can not only color a people's outlook and affect their behavior, but also do so more effectively than involuted histories, philosophies, and works of realistic fiction.

What, I wonder, did Tolstoy think of "The Grand Inquisitor," a chapter in *The Brothers Karamazov* (1880), by Fyodor Dostoevsky (1821–1881)? We know that Tolstoy was not wholly sympathetic with Dostoevsky's oeuvre, including much of its underlying theology, but wouldn't he have approved of that particular chapter, which is presented as a fable? The fable tells of the return of Christ to Earth at the time when the Spanish Inquisition was at its height. The Grand Inquisitor put Christ in prison on the ground that he threatened to undo what the official church was providing the people: "miracle, mystery, and authority." These were the things the people needed, the Grand Inquisitor argued, and not Christ's ideal, which only a few spiritual athletes could pursue. Should ordinary men and women try, they would only end in disillusionment and misery. The Grand Inquisitor, who put many to death because they threatened the peace he sought to bring, could have put Christ to death, too. But he didn't. Instead, he allowed his prisoner to leave with the warning that he must never return.

Throughout the Grand Inquisitor's harangue, Christ said not a word, nor did he when the prison door stood open for him. Christ's last gesture—indeed, his only real one during the brief revisit to Earth—was to plant a kiss on the Inquisitor's "bloodless, ninety-year-old lips."[29]

The fable is memorable. What stays in the memory is not any moral prescription but rather two strong personalities set against each other: silent Christ versus the articulate Grand Inquisitor; a single kiss versus the projection of institutionalized power; a goodness that is barely of this world versus one that is steeped in it. The reader of the fable is made to identify with one or the other of these two personalities. Whichever the reader chooses reveals a deep-seated proclivity in his or her own moral stance. To have that moral stance so vividly revealed may affect the reader in one of two ways: enforce it or, just possibly, change one's path.

Among the most influential stories in the world are those told about charismatic figures such as Gautama Buddha, Bodhisattva Kwan-yin (the deity of mercy and compassion), Jesus Christ, and St. Francis of Assisi. Miracles are scattered through the narratives, which make them fables, not true biographies. Yet their timeless appeal is indisputable, answering something deep in our nature. But what is it? We have no trouble naming the basic physical needs of food, shelter, and sex, nor the basic social needs of care, respect, and love. Can there also be a spiritual need that goes beyond even love as it is commonly understood to something for which the words that most readily come to mind are goodness, the Good, or God? Absent food, shelter, and sex, we die. Absent care, respect, and love, we live—barely. Absent that deep and insatiable spiritual yearning for the Good that certain stories and fables prefigure? We live, and indeed we may live well, in full, societal approbation and self-congratulatory glow, except, perhaps, in those uncanny moments—the sudden chill in the air, a pinched feeling in the heart, or even a stumble over the curb that reminds us of the abyss beneath the pavement on which we so unconcernedly walk.

Fables and even fairy tales cannot be pure fantasies, for they are made of words, and words inevitably evoke objects and events in real life. Music, not being denotative, comes closest to being pure fantasy. Can music have a moral effect, as I believe fables can? The Greeks spoke of the musical harmony of the spheres, with the implication that harmony in the heavens could carry over to the human sphere. Ancient China held a similar idea.[30] Still, on the whole, moral philosophers ignore music or see it in a morally negative light, considering it an emotional indulgence, a threat to reason. The philosopher William James urged that one does something good after attending the opera, even if it is to help an old lady cross the street; otherwise, one risks becoming morally flabby.[31] Iris Murdoch (1919–1999) doesn't even mention music in her subtle disquisitions on the Good. Her interest is exclusively on words, which alone have that degree of specificity, that power to draw attention to detail, that is a hallmark of goodness.[32]

I am unsure where my own position lies. Beethoven's music pumps up my adrenaline and gives me courage. Nevertheless, it is a mere feeling unless I put it to the test. Music by Johannes Brahms (1833–1897) makes me feel melancholic, a mood that just might make me a little more sympathetic, though, I fear, only for a moment. Certain music—*Symphony No. 4*, known as *The Italian Symphony* (1833), by Felix Mendelssohn (1809–1847), for example—makes me happy. And what is happiness? I see it as more than just a feeling; it can be a contagious moral state that uplifts anyone who happens to be nearby. People who have "music" in their soul are fun to be with.

I speak of pure music—instrumental music. Music set to words gives me a stronger sense of moral direction. When I listen to J. S. Bach's *Mass in B Minor* (1749) and *War Requiem* (1961) by Benjamin Britten (1913–1976), I no longer ask, "Which of the two sublimities—music or words—has the greater moral uplift?" They are inseparable: words alone lack the visceral punch; music alone risks becoming a swooning emotion. Now, let me add a personal note. Earlier, I mentioned Tolstoy's high regard for his simple stories and fables as against his monumental novels. He has in mind, I believe, their relative moral influence. It occurs to me that's how I respond to music. I am enthralled by the great masterpieces of classical music, but, when it comes to moral influence, old hymns such as "Be Still My Soul" and "When I Survey the Wondrous Cross" are more likely to make me yearn to be a better human being.[33]

For all the beauties of nature, all the marvels of human creation, and all the exemplary acts of human goodness, we humans appear to have learned little. We continue to bear the defects of our nature (the "sins"), and we continue to harm our own kind and all of God's creation. What is wrong with us? To put the puzzle a little differently, "How is it that, for all the keenness of our senses and mind, we still all too often live in a state of stupor, with eyes that look but do not see, with ears that hear but do not understand?"

Of course, there were and are exceptions—individuals who have kept humanity at a certain level of moral alertness. In Part V, I return to the individual, whom I have never really left, for the individual hovers in the background even when the foreground is the group.

PART V

The Individual

CHAPTER 14

The Indivudual vs. the Group:
Particularity vs. Oneness

H UMANISM AT THE TIME OF THE RENAISSANCE asked the
question, "What is man?" and gave answers that elevated
human dignity. No longer under the subjection of the
hierarchies, both cosmic and human, that was the rule in medieval times, one
was free to find oneself in nature and in society. A consequence of Renaissance
humanism was that it initiated a growing appreciation of the individual. But,
in later times, a counter-movement, which came to be known as the "social
sciences," chose to underplay the individual as against the group. Human geography, which emphasizes *place* and *community*, might be considered a part of
that movement. The discipline has people but almost no individual with a personal name. In using the expression "humanist geography," then, I juxtapose
two words that highlight their mutually supportive yet also tense and even
antagonistic relationship.

The geographer, the social scientist, and the sociobiologist all might ask,
"Why the individual?" From their viewpoint the group's importance can be
taken for granted, for it is, after all, the unit of survival and the unit through
which genetic material is passed on. But why pay attention to a single member
unless he or she is, in some way, exceptional? The word "exceptional" in itself
can make some of us uneasy, for it calls to mind its opposites—"ordinary" and
"common"—raising the specter that people are not equal. There are different
kinds of inequality, however, since inequality applies to different gifts, abilities,
and circumstances. Socioeconomic inequality is tolerable to the extent that we
can work to mitigate and even remove it. Inequality in natural gifts and in the
accidents of fortune is beyond our power to control or rectify. For that reason,
it can be deeply disturbing. Some of us are so dismayed by the unfairness of
life that we are driven to entertain the idea of life continuing beyond death, not
from weak flesh's desire to survive as from a deep psycho-spiritual need that
there be ultimate restitution and justice.

Some form of belief in life beyond death is common among humans. Our
prehistoric ancestors showed their hope for bodily survival in their burial cus-

toms, all the world's major religions subscribe to some notion of life continuing beyond the cessation of breath, and Christianity does so specifically in its doctrine of the resurrection and the Last Judgment. Can the belief be innate to our nature?[1]

I ask, because even modern secularists and atheists cannot quite shed the notion. They seem to believe that, upon death, their spirit will somehow linger to be embarrassed by pornographic magazines under the mattress or that it will posthumously see their poems receive the acclaim they deserve. One might expect modern science to douse the idea of immortality, but it hasn't quite happened—yet. Indeed, it can raise new hope, as it had in the Union of Soviet Socialist Republics (1922–1991) in Eurasia, which is surprising, for, if any country can be counted on to dismiss "life everlasting," it would be the former Soviet Union (U.S.S.R.). Yet, for two reasons, something like its promotion occurred. One is the lingering influence of the Christian worldview in the works of Russian writers and artists, an influence so strong that even a "political" writer such as Maxim Gorky (1868–1936) couldn't altogether escape. The other is the inclination of Marxist thinkers to attribute unlimited power to science. Science, in Soviet orthodoxy, is a story of the conquest of nature. One by one the limits that nature placed on the human path have fallen. The logic of success prevents Marxists from admitting that nature's ultimate "no"—death—is insurmountable.[2]

Immortality was seen, historically, as the attribute of a social class. The elite could aspire to it, the common people could not. The latter, never having amounted to much in this life, were expected to return to dust after death. Some such belief was taken for granted in all civilizations, including the Western. Take ancient Greece. It had a number of distinguishing features. One was its encouragement of its elite to act out of personal conviction—in other words, as individuals; another, related to this incipient individualism, was that the ancient Greeks, more than other peoples, not only distinguished between private and public life, but gave each a moral tone in which the former, however comfortable and dignified, was deemed unworthy of a citizen. (Note that the Greek word *idios*—our word "idiot"—meant "private.") To prove his mettle, the citizen had to present himself in the city (*polis* = policy = public) and there engage his peers in speech and action for the common good.

Life in the private sphere of farm and homestead did not require courage, since the activities there had no other purpose than biological survival and material well-being. Life in the public sphere did occasionally call for courage. A speech in the forum and even in the marketplace, when given with conviction, might offend a powerful rival. A man could find himself ostracized, exiled, and even put to death. On the other hand, should his speech—his act— be recorded, the offender, for all his earthly trials, just might achieve immortal fame. The same possibility was open to the heroic warrior. He might die a cruel death on the battlefield, struck down by a rival or a whim of the gods; but, if the deed were recorded, his reputation could live forever.

The private sphere, though it catered to the necessities and comforts of life, was not free from lacerating experience. Far from it. The gods could as easily exercise their arbitrary will there as they could in the public realm. Human passions, moreover, might erupt all the more violently in the tight spaces and dark corners of a domicile. Sensing the injustice of allowing such events to sink into oblivion for lack of a scribe to record them, the Greeks came up with a solution: they created an art form called tragedy. Tragedy served two purposes. As theater, it produced catharsis in those who knew the horrors; as play, it gave private horrors—the passions of the bedroom—the dignity of visibility and permanence.[3]

What about the common people? In all times, the elite barely recognized them as individuals with minds of their own. They could, of course, react to circumstance and do so violently, but they weren't credited with the ability to act in the sense of initiating. Incapable of genuine action, much less the grand gesture, they were ipso facto also incapable of catastrophic failure and tragedy. Historically, the lower orders were treated as nonentities. If they had a purpose in life, it was to perform society's menial chores as unobtrusively as possible. When not so occupied? Well, they might provide comic relief to their betters, thanks to their uncomely faces and ungainly behavior.

Shakespeare's tragedies exemplified this attitude. In *Romeo and Juliet*, the hero and the heroine belonged to the upper bourgeoisie; one had to be at least of that rank to rise to tragic grandeur, and, in fact, the social class of Shakespeare's tragic figures seldom fell below that of nobility. The powerless—Juliet's nurse, for one—were droll figures. And they remained so in literature and art until well into the 1800s. Even late in the nineteenth century, cartoonists in *Punch* pretty much restricted pratfalls and other clumsy behavior to the indigent and unwashed. That they nevertheless had immortal souls must be accepted, for such was the teaching of the official church. But the powerful could hardly have taken the teaching to heart, for they habitually regarded the teeming masses as lacking personhood and individuality, basic requirements for possessing an immortal soul.[4]

THE GROUP AND THE INDIVIDUAL IN THE BIBLE

Whether we look at immortality or at individuality, the West has always labored under a moral contradiction: on the one hand, people do not matter; on the other hand, they do, each man and woman being unique and irreplaceable. This contradiction is already in full display in the *Bible*. With remarkable nonchalance God wiped out those who displeased Him—men, women, and children—to make way for those who enjoyed His favor. Treating outsiders with the greatest severity, including death, was commonplace. Treating members of one's own group in like offhand manner should be rare. But was it? The Book of Job has stimulated many commentaries, most of which are directed at the unjust suffering of Job. Skipped by them is how God tested Job by depriving him of his children. Job's children were not hostile outsiders. They belonged to the community and had done no wrong, so why were they killed? No one raised the question, much less proffered an answer. When God found that Job remained faithful, He graciously rewarded him by replacing his dead offspring with another batch, freshly baked, as it were, from the oven. What the story shows is that the children were not regarded as individuals, each a work of divine art; like cattle, they could be replaced.

An altogether different view of individual human worth also appears in the *Bible* in the story of Amos. Amos was a nobody, just a sheepherder living a few miles outside Bethlehem. God, however, chose him to tell the truth to the idolatrous Israelites. And the truth was this: to serve God means to act with justice and not with burnt offerings and long-winded prayers. The latter is easily done, a matter of following routine procedures, but the former implies the existence of an inner self that recognizes the inherent rightness and beauty of justice. Who possesses the inner self? Before Amos, who lived during the eighth century BCE, it was believed that God created the inner self (a self in possession of "spirit" or *ruach*) only in important people, such as prophets, priests, and kings. The radicalism of true prophets—Amos, Jeremiah, and Ezekiel—was to extend that "inside" to all people. Each man was to be a king, a prophet, or a priest in his own right.[5]

If each person can achieve greatness, so can each fall into baseness. A great king can be a bad king, seeking his own glory rather than the common good; a great prophet can be a false prophet, blinding his followers with partial truths. Moreover, each is a title, an official position. Each, in other words, is thoroughly embedded in a social milieu, which itself can be corrupt and corrupting. Given the *ruach* in each of us, given that we all have an inner (and higher, God-like) self, we should all be able to strive toward a goal more worthy than greatness, which is all too often just unbridled ambition. And that more worthy project is goodness or the Good.

EASTERN RELIGIONS VS. CHRISTIANITY

To strive, however, implies desire. Strong desire is seen in a positive light in the West so long as its object is the Good (ancient Greece) and God (Christendom). Eastern thought is more ambivalent. Buddhism famously teaches that desire is the source of all illusion and of all suffering. Put thus, desire could almost be deemed the source of all evil. To escape illusion and suffering, one must be purged of yearning—a long and difficult process that may take many incarnations to attain. What state does one enter when one finally succeeds? The answer is nirvana. In nirvana, one no longer desires; indeed one is no longer a "one," a circumscribed self.[6]

Buddhist nirvana is grounded in Hinduism, an older belief system. Hinduism, as expressed in the *Upanishads* (800–400 BCE), teaches that the individual has something at its core called *atman*, which is the human correlate of Brahman or ultimate reality. The human individual, despite the presence of *atman* at its core, lives in a state of illusion. Upon an individual's death, all that remains is *atman*, which rejoins Brahman. An image common to both Hinduism and Buddhism is of a river flowing into the sea.

The West has inherited this way of thinking by way of Plato, whose metaphysic is believed to have been affected by Hindu thought.[7] Plato uses, however, a different image. The world we live in and perceive through the senses, he says, is distorted. Reality consists of eternal Forms or Ideas that are inaccessible to the senses. Plato also gives us the image of the cave: we live in a cave and see only shadows when reality is the blistering sun. Christianity has found Platonic thought sympathetic, for, to Christian thinkers, the world is a fallen world in which its human habitants are enslaved by vanities and delusions. God, or rather the Godhead, is something quite Other, abstract just as Forms and Ideas are abstract, and can no more than the sun be directly seen by mortal eyes. To St. Augustine of Hippo (354–430), an early and highly influential Christian Platonist, God alone is unchanging reality, and all the rest—the particulars—change or are ephemeral. Unlike Plato, however, St. Augustine finds himself distressingly attached to one category of particulars—his friends. Another important difference is that St. Augustine's God can be prayed to. The views I have just sketched are still very much alive. Platonism continues to flourish in mathematical thinkers of our day, outstandingly, in Jan Lukasiewicz (1878–1958) and Roger Penrose (b. 1931). Their God, however, cannot be prayed to. Simone Weil's God can. Her thought is a crystalline distillation of ideas from Platonism, Hinduism, and Christianity.

Aristotle is the other powerful early influence on Western philosophy. His viewpoint is the opposite of Plato's. To Aristotle, the real are the substantive particulars: this horse, this table, and not the idea of a horse and the idea of a table. Christianity finds Aristotle sympathetic, too, for a strain of Christian thought harps on God as Creator and sees the variety and richness of His creation as redounding to His glory. Thomas Aquinas (1225–1274) is the most important Aristotelian in the history of Christian theology. To him, things, for all their defects, are truly present and actual and far more real than any thought or dream. In the real presence of things, he finds signs of God's creative power.[8] In our day, C. S. Lewis is a well-known Christian Aristotelian, who sees the warts and blisters of creation yet chooses to remind us of its fundamental glory and goodness. He does so in his scholarly writings, in his Christian apologetics, and, perhaps most effectively, in his seven-volume Narnian Chronicles (1949–1954), which are fables for young and old.

Where do I stand? Given my educational background in the West, it is not surprising that I embrace both Plato and Aristotle as well as their intellectual descendants, even though they are in opposite camps. More precisely, I embrace Plato and the *Upanishads* in one mood and Aristotle and Christian thinkers, such as Thomas Aquinas, in another. I yearn not only to be in metaphysical flight, but also to come fully to life in the world of particulars. In what follows, I will forgo the first path, which is always in danger of becoming anti-humanist, and develop the second, which, in its emphasis on individuals and their potential, is at the core of humanism.

ENVISAGING HEAVEN

Reality, in the Aristotelian view, consists of individual things—"shoes, ships, and sealing wax, cabbages and kings," as Lewis Carroll put it.[9] Sick or in low spirits, these particulars lose their vividness and sharp outlines. If we fear death, it is because we have developed an attachment to the particulars—above all, our loved ones—and dread the oblivion, the absorption into oceanic oneness, that awaits us. As an alternative to oblivion, various religions, outstandingly Christianity and Islam, postulate a heaven on the other side of the great divide. What heaven is like has never been successful portrayed. All too often it is a pale imitation of the good place in this life—a happier hunting ground, a village or town of well-appointed houses and streets, a perfect garden, a peaceful valley. The West's imagination is hardly more powerful. Among the two most popular images are a pastoral scene of saints adoring God with choral singing and, inspired by the Book of Revelation, a bejeweled celestial city.

Why is hell so much easier to envisage? Can it be that a place of torture has to be specific for the perpetual pain and misery to feel real, whereas, contrarily, a place of bliss has to be non-specific, something more like a flow of light, color, and music, if it is not to seem pedestrian, earthbound? But to see a place of bliss thus abstractly moves us too close to the metaphysical and Buddhist ultimate state of being, when what we strive to picture is a heaven of glorious particulars. Is it possible?

One solution—to my mind, the only possible one—is to approach the challenge indirectly: don't try to picture heaven; rather suggest the *possibility* of a place that is more real and solid than the one we know. I offer two illustrations of how indirection works. The first is a fable by C. S. Lewis. The second is a story of my own invention, plausibly true, which I have modified from one that was told by the neurologist Sir Russell Brain (1895–1966).

Lewis's fable begins with passengers pushing to get on a bus, although there was no need to push since plenty of seats were available. They were to take a holiday from their town, which made sense, for it was a miserable place of tacky houses and stores perpetually drenched in rain and mist. The bus climbed up a long, steep slope, and, as it got higher, the dank and murky atmosphere was left behind for lighter and cleaner air. Rather than being pleased with the change, the passengers spent much time whining and complaining, until the bus reached over the edge of a cliff and came to a stop. They had arrived. One passenger—the only one who did not whine—saw from the bus window a grassy, tree-dotted landscape bathed in early morning sunshine. He looked at his fellow passengers and was astonished to find that they were nearly transparent, like blotches of dirt on a window pane, and that, when they stepped out of the bus and stood on the grass, the grass barely bent—even the dew on them was undisturbed. He concluded that the blades must be extremely hard, like stainless steel, and that it would be excruciatingly painful to walk on them; moreover, should it rain, the raindrops would penetrate him like bullets. It was not a place for him and his fellow tourists, all shadowy beings, unless they could somehow be made more real and solid. At that moment bright, laughing people, young and old, came running onto the grass, their bare feet flattening the blades, releasing a sweet scent into the air.[10]

The next story sees a British warship moving stealthily along the coast of Norway during World War II (1939–1945). It has to move either in total darkness or in a thick fog so as not to attract attention from a country that was ruled by Nazi Germany (1933–1945). Fortunately, this could be done, for radar had recently been invented. The ship's radar was a luminous screen not much larger than a dinner plate. Patches of light and shadow appeared on the screen, and with this information—and only this information—the navigator could safely steer the vessel along the intricately indented coastline. After a few days below deck, almost everyone came to believe that the flashes of light on the screen constituted all there was of reality. And why not? The ship was on course; it did not smash into an island or a sea cliff. So imagine the crew's astonishment when, one bright day, they climbed out of the hull to the deck and found a world that they had almost forgotten—an overarching blue sky with fluffy, white clouds, a fjord coast draped in waterfalls, air scented by sea spray, and seagulls crying shrilly overhead. The crew felt as though they awoke from a long and troubled sleep.[11]

The merit of these two stories is that it reminds us that the reality we know is a gift of our senses which, as I indicated earlier, are powerful and far-ranging. Yet they are also limited. For example, we can't see infrared light, but what if we can? And what if our nose is as discriminating as that of a dog? Reality will then be different, and it can be richer—far richer. Secondly, we grossly underuse the senses we do have, constrained by environment, culture, and our own stupidity—our fallen nature.

CHAPTER 15

Am I Real? Do I Matter?

T O FALLEN CREATURES, Earth can seem a tacky suburb. In really bad moments, it can even seem as circumscribed and dull as what appears on a radar screen. The fallen creatures themselves are little more than shadows—a view that may be a bit extreme, but it is not implausible from both subjective and objective angles.

Subjectively, I feel, at times, unreal, empty at the core. This is one reason I stuff my pantry with food and my closets with purchases that I might not even open. Material things do not, however, sufficiently buttress my sense of self. Even more, I need other humans, the test of which is that I never feel more listless, as though I have no center or purpose, than when I am alone. Having someone to talk with is reassuring, but it is a tenuous sort of reassurance, vanishing the moment his eyes glaze over with boredom or when I catch him glancing over my shoulder to locate a person of more substance. Even when I am in someone's sight, I may not be in his mind. And when I am out of his sight? Suppose I go away for a year or two. The smile he gives me upon my return does not seem quite sincere—understandably, for my return will cause him the inconvenience of readjusting his settled routines.[1]

I use the first-person singular, but I believe we all are barely real to ourselves; we all need others to confirm our existence, hungry for their nods of recognition, resentful of their averted eye or look of indifference. And, as I wrote earlier, when confronted by authority we quickly lose self-respect. So much for the psychological states—the subjective viewpoints. What is a more objective, scientific viewpoint? It is no more reassuring. Science sees us as animals that differ from apes only in a few anatomical details. Moreover, science belittles us with numbers. It says, for example, that biological evolution has produced in 4,000,000,000 years billions of species, 99.9 percent of which are extinct.[2] True, we humans are among the survivors, but that's hardly an argument for our importance. A better one is that we are the most complex organism to have emerged on Earth, in the solar system, and, perhaps even, in the galaxy. So regarded we as a species are of some import, but then why worry about the fate of one individual or even of thousands and tens of thousands of individuals when they are still a tiny portion of the total human population and can, moreover, be quickly replaced?

One fact is well established, which is: though I may at times belittle my own worth and even that of the species, I nevertheless maintain a strong partiality toward my own group. My survival depends on the partiality. Distinguishing between "us" and "them" and routinely favoring the "us" is so widespread that it may well be a bias encoded in the brain. All the more unexpected, then, is the emergence of the idea that certain basic human rights extend far beyond one's own group to other groups and not only to other groups, but to every human individual.[3] This idea, though formulated with panache and clarity during the Age of Reason, has, in fact, no support in reason or science. Its roots are various and deep, the most important of which are the great world religions and philosophies. They have in common the belief that the human being possesses an inner core, called variously *atman*, spirit (*ruach*), or soul. We are all alike and entitled to respect by virtue of this possession.

How can one tell that there is this spirit or soul inside every person? True, the prophet Amos said so, as did Socrates and Plato, as did Christian preachers and a number of modern moralists. But, for all the authority of such figures, the idea did not take hold other than in regard to the powerful and the privileged. Only during the eighteenth century did a change of attitude begin to emerge. What brought it about? The development of gentler manners and, with it, a greater sensitivity to the feeling of others? The spread of education, reading, and curiosity? One source of change could be the rising popularity of the novel. The first novels appeared two centuries earlier, but they did not explore the inner life of the humble, as their successors were more inclined to do. In consequence of this exploration, the reading public—a growing number by the 1800s—was prepared to see their maids and footmen, and not just their friends, as complex human beings. Such a way of seeing marked a significant moral advance, but it took a while to penetrate the population. As I have noted, throughout much of the nineteenth century the print media and the theater continued to depict the "great unwashed" as all surface and no depths, cartoonish stereotypes.[4]

CHAPTER 16

Equality and Inequality

HAVING AN INNER LIFE and spirit gives humans a dignity above that of other animals, but it doesn't automatically make them good. Quite the contrary. Lucifer had spirit, but it only made him worse, just as humans all too often behave far worse than do animals. Spirit may be considered a general endowment that empowers one to go either way—good or evil. The same holds for the more specific endowments, such as physical strength, intelligence, and beauty: strength makes for courage, intelligence enables one to see hidden truths, and beauty shines, bringing happiness to the world. But the reverse is as likely to happen: strength tempts one to bullying, intelligence tempts one to mere cleverness, and beauty tempts one to vanity.

Still, despite the ambivalence, strength, intelligence, and beauty are highly desirable gifts. The question then arises, "How are they distributed?" That the distribution is uneven is all too evident: without doubt some individuals are stronger, brighter, or better looking than are others. The Judeo-Christian tradition has little to say about these endowments, their ranking, and the justness of their distribution. The one endowment it does have much to say is goodness. Goodness trumps all other gifts, if only because it is incapable of perversion or misuse, at least not consciously, for to do so consciously would contradict the very idea of goodness. Goodness also trumps beauty in that a homely person can be good, even supremely good. The prophet Isaiah (53: 2) was the first to make this point, and Christianity took it up by making Isaiah's man with "no form nor comliness" a prefiguration of Christ: "…and when we shall see him, there is no beauty that we should desire him."[1]

What this means is that, in Judeo-Christian thought, beauty doesn't matter much. Ancient Greeks would have been appalled. To them—and even to Socrates, who was ugly—beauty mattered greatly. And the world agrees with the Greeks: social scientists have shown again and again that good looks make a real difference in how one fares in the world. So it is Judeo-Christian thought that is out of line, and even there the superior value of goodness over beauty has never received much emphasis: it has never been made an official doctrine to be propagated from the pulpits. Moreover, shifting value from beauty to goodness doesn't solve the problem of inequality. Goodness is as unequally distributed as any other endowment. This particular inequality hasn't jarred moral sensibility for at least two reasons: one is that a good person is only too likely to suffer for being good; and the other is that degrees of goodness are of little account, for the standard by which all are judged is nothing less than perfection, "Be ye therefore perfect, even as your Father which is in heaven is perfect" (Matthew 5: 48). By that standard, all fall far short.

The biological inequalities are plain to see. Another source of inequality, also plain to see and which we also ignore, is geography. By 10,000 BCE, humans could be found in all parts of Earth, the only exceptions being the polar ice caps and the highest mountains. Now, humans weren't there by choice; they landed in one environment rather than in another as the result of natural events and the accidents of life. Environments differ greatly in resources. At one extreme are the ice fields and deserts; at the other extreme are the mid-latitude forests and tropical islands. No matter how adaptive people are, life is still harsh in the one and easy in the other. Where, then, is the justice? There can be no conceivable answer, and yet, if we are serious about human inequalities, we cannot arbitrarily rule out those imposed by biology and physical geography.

Socioeconomic inequalities can be reduced, and we have tried to do so from time to time, especially during the last century when the question of social justice succeeded in wakening more consciences. Still, the efforts have not been wholehearted. Selfishness and laziness—the ineradicable underside of human nature—are one reason. The inefficiencies and corruptions inherent to complex institutions charged to redistribute wealth are another. A third might be Christianity itself. The religion, after all, carries Jesus's warning, "...It is easier for a camel to go through the eye of a needle than for a rich man to enter the kingdom of God" (Matthew 19: 24). Wealth so bloats one's girth that passing through the Pearly Gate is impossible. The saying can also be interpreted to mean that the rich, having had all the blessings of this life, are not entitled to those in the next.

Both readings suggest that the kingdom lies elsewhere. The gospels, however, are never entirely clear on this point. They sometimes seem to say that God's kingdom is heaven—a place other than Earth—but, at other times, they seem to say that it is where we are now, only we don't have the eyes to see. If the kingdom is—in some sense—already here in God's earthly creation, what *would* we see if we had unclouded vision? Well, for one, the lilies of the field, whose glory is unmatched even by Solomon's raiments (Matthew 6: 28–29). And, of course, there are many other charms and beauties in nature, and in artifacts as well, to see and embrace. Given the existence of these good things, which are more or less available to everyone, we may have to conclude that, even in this life, there is more justice than we recognize. Our failure to recognize it lies in our habit of mistaking legal ownership for true possession, economics for aesthetics.

True possession is to have whatever the world offers as an integral part of one's life experience, and that can only happen when one is *able* to experience—that is, to see, feel, and understand truly. Legal ownership, though it does not exclude possession in the above sense, nevertheless diminishes its likelihood. The reason is that the proper appreciation of many goods takes time and effort, which the rich may be unable or unwilling to expend, and so they end up with the easier satisfaction of mere ownership. The rich's ability to enjoy what they have is also limited by the fact that they are biological beings. They can eat only three meals a day and sleep in one bed at a time. Even the quality of what they do enjoy may not be so different from that which is available to ordinary folks. The rich can, for example, eat off Sèvres plates, but food doesn't necessarily taste better when it is served on pedigreed chinaware. Sinking into puffy pillows and immaculate bed sheets is a luxury for the rich, but the sensation is no greater than what a workman enjoys as he collapses onto a bunk bed or, in degree of voluptuousness, as a poor student can know when she sinks into the arms of the beloved. The cool water that a landscape gardener drinks after hard work is surely as much a delight as the wine that the rich sip between mouthfuls of quail meat.[2] Moreover, children—even those of the poor—may be said to possess Mother Earth by virtue of their openness and natural vitality. Jesus says repeatedly that the kingdom of God belongs to the children, and we can believe him when we see boys and girls skip, hop, and jump even under a threatening sky. We grown-ups haven't forgotten these ecstasies entirely. Our fancy houses and cars, our trips to Nepal and Machu Picchu notwithstanding, we still look back to our childhood's sensorial cornucopia with a sense of loss and longing.

Experience takes time and calls for patience. Under the compulsion to build up wealth and under wealth's demand for quantification, the rich acutely feel time's shortage. An investment tycoon calculates that, since every hour he is on the phone, he can make an extra $100,000 for his company, it is absurd for him to use that hour in an art gallery, the admission fee to which is trifling. Much more in line with his wealth is to buy a painting for a few million dollars and put it in the bank vault as an investment. And, again, rather than go to the symphony and have his soul filled with sublime music, the tycoon may feel that his time is more rationally spent gaining prestige through sending a large check to the arts foundation of which he is the chairman. As for the beauties of nature, they cost even less to visit and take even longer to enjoy. And so our tycoon stays in his wood-paneled office, sits in a swivel chair next to potted plants, and writes another large check, this time made out to the Nature Conservancy.

There is something heroic, even saintly, about such a life. A person with less money and subject to less time constraint can lead a life that is self-indulgent by comparison. I, for one, would gladly spend a few hours in the Museum of Modern Art in New York City, or an evening listening to the interminable but lush orchestration of *Symphony No. 9* (1912), by Gustav Mahler (1860–1910), or even a weekend ascent into the ancient settlement atop the high mesa at

Acoma Pueblo ("Sky City") in west-central New Mexico. Economic inequality turns out to work in my favor.[3]

UNEQUAL LIFE SPAN

Life span is greatly unequal: taking the world as a whole, many die young, and relatively few live to extreme old age. How long one lives is partially dependent on one's genes. Unlike beauty and natural talent, it also depends very much on social and economic conditions. Even today, the rich live longer than the poor, and the gap was far greater in the past. Extending a life span is a good that we can and would want to do something about. A major project of the World Health Organization is to raise life expectancy in the developing countries. But is longevity as such an unqualified good? Shouldn't quality matter as much, if not more, than quantity? Much of life is, after all, stressful, or so one must assume from the many who seek to numb it with alcohol, drugs, and frivolous pastimes. As for a very long life, the last scene—a vegetative existence "sans teeth, sans eyes, sans taste, sans everything"—is more cruel and unusual punishment than a blessing.

Attitude toward longevity and toward life itself varies from people to people. The Chinese and the Greeks appear to be at opposite poles. The Chinese make a cult of longevity: the character for long life (*shou*) is displayed in many homes, shops, and restaurants. I can understand the Chinese yearning, but only because, until a generation or two ago, life expectancy in China was so low. The ancient Greeks baffle me far more by seeming to desire the opposite. One of them, Sophocles (496–406 BCE), said what no Chinese sage could ever have said: "Best is not to be born; second best is to die young."[4] Die young? Die in childhood? Such an event is, to us moderns, shocking, unnatural, and against the right order of things. And yet, by making death in childhood *too* dark, we risk undervaluing the short life that was lived. It is worth remembering that the first few years are packed with wonders that rarely recur in adulthood.

What wonders? One is a world in which the wind sings, the water sparkles, the lambs dance, and human artifacts—even one as common as an eraser-tipped pencil—are a marvel of ingenuity and craftsmanship. Another is the ever curious mind. Even if we end as dull professionals and politicians, we begin as spirited philosophers, bombarding our parents with endless whys. "Are these flowers still alive?" asks the child as her mother puts them in a vase.[5] Well, are they, or are they corpses?

What about wisdom? We say "a wise child" as we say "a wise fool," using the word to mean a proclivity to tell the truth. Truth telling—or, if we prefer, a certain bluntness—comes naturally to children and fools, because their thinking is less socially conditioned. But "wise" also implies a special insight into life and death. That insight, I once thought, is reserved for the mature. After reading Myra Blueblond-Langner's book on dying leukemic children, I am not so sure. The book contains examples of children's extraordinary realism, thoughtfulness, and even humor in the face of imminent death. A six-year-old boy wakes up from a long nap and sees two interns by his bed. The boy says with a smile, "I fooled you, I didn't die."[6]

And, then, there is knowledge. Adults certainly know much more than children, but what is it worth? At times, I think that most of what we adults know is dross, resembling what one might find in a dumpster—empty beer cans and wine bottles, old telephone directories and pornographic magazines, uneaten pizzas and used contraceptives, twisted coat hangers and soiled underwear.

CHAPTER 17

Progress Considered
One More Time

A CHILD, FOR ALL SHE OR HE KNOWS OF JOY, A child, for
all she or he knows of joy, will not know experiences
unique to maturity: sexual ecstasy, parenthood, great
art and literature, the wonders of the universe. Even so, this is not the final
word, for experience does not necessarily accumulate such that, as one follows
another, life is progressively enriched. To the contrary, one good experience
may well *displace* another: when I am ready for sexual ecstasy, I lose my boy-
ish delight in friendship; parenthood is a huge gain, but it is achieved at the
expense of the so-called unfettered freedom of the single state; appreciating the
subtleties of art and literature makes me nostalgic for the innocent pleasure in
catchy tunes and the passionate devouring of adventure stories. Additionally,
as one grows older, the inevitable reverses of life run parallel with the successes
and joys, casting a shadow over them, so they never quite reach childhood's
shining peaks.

J. M. Barrie's Peter Pan (1902) wants to be a boy forever, dreading the stale
routines of maturity. He has a point. In working-class families of Edward-
ian England, Peter's age peers have fixed identities by the time they enter the
work force, which may be as young as seven or eight. Maturity is delayed in
the middle- and upper-middle class families; nevertheless, youths often settle
into a profession that defines their identity by their late teen or early twenties,
and there they stay for the rest of their working lives. Ambition is directed at a
bigger salary, a higher position in the corporation, and a bigger house, but the
house of intellect, which they have pretty much finished building by the time
they enter or graduate from college, remains much the same. People who feel
constrained if they do not move from the small apartment of their student days
to the multi-roomed residence of maturity appear to be comfortable living all
their adult life within the walls of their first ill-put-together intellectual house.
People want to improve themselves; they want to make progress. Surprising is
the almost total emphasis on social status and material plenty, as though these,

rather than the quality of their mind and spirit, define what they have accomplished and who they truly are.

Old age is the age of iron rather than the gold promised by life insurance companies. Both body and mind lose their suppleness and shine. Sentimentally, one might think that, in the twilight years, one becomes at least more kindly disposed, having left behind life's ambition and struggles. Sad to say, even this scenario is too rosy. If the old are benign on certain occasions, it may have more to do with good digestion and a good night's sleep than with accumulated wisdom. As disabilities mount and even putting on the trousers is a heroic struggle, the old—under constant stress—become more self-centered, irritable, inflexible, and demanding. These traits are nonetheless adaptive, for, according to gerontologist John Grimely Evans, old people must continue to be engaged to remain healthy, and the easiest way for them to be engaged is to be curmudgeons.[1]

Is there progress in culture and society? Most people, to the extent they have contemplated the temporal process, believe that it changed little or that is showed evidence of decline or was cyclical. A few individuals had views about socioeconomic development that implied progress. For example, ancient Greece had Xenophanes (c. 570–c. 475 BCE), who said that the gods didn't reveal all things from the beginning; rather, men had to find what was better through their own search. Ancient China, too, entertained the idea of progress. It had Mencius (371 or 372–289 BCE), who recognized commerce as a new source of wealth. More generally, the Chinese of his time and later saw progress in the refinement of manners and in the literary arts. In Europe, humanists during the Renaissance certainly believed in man's upward path. They had no doubt that their culture and society were superior to those of the medieval period, and, for evidence, they could point not only to better social manners and greater concision in language, but also to the introduction of perspective in painting, polyphony in music, and the numerous innovations in technical and scientific fields. Despite these earlier instances, it was during the eighteenth century—the Age of Enlightenment—that the idea of progress found truly broad acceptance among the educated and the well-to-do, and it remained broadly accepted until the twilight years of the nineteenth century. For a variety of reasons, doubt then entered, becoming more corrosive with time and peaking in the horrors of World War I (1914–1918).

Where do I fit in? I was born in 1930, well after the onset of a more pessimistic mood in the Western world; and yet, despite having lived through World War II as a child, I continue to be attracted to the idea of progress, even on questions of morality, though with reservations. This, then, is how I see progress—and regress. For most of human time, only kinfolk and neighbors merited help. Strangers did not receive it because they could not be counted on to give it in return. In the more advanced societies, they were viewed more sympathetically, if only because trade required friendly contact with people one did not know. As the network of trade expanded, so did the network of friendship. Travel over the thinly populated, brigand-infested roads entailed risk. It may be that, in ancient Greece, the supreme god Zeus was invented so that those who left the city walls and the aegis of the local deities could stay under some form of protection.[2] In any case, homesteads and farms along the way were expected to offer hospitality. Not offering it would have been considered a serious moral lapse.

All major religions—Buddhism, Judaism, Christianity, and Islam—made kindness to strangers a moral precept. In time, a combination of factors—long-distance trade, safety on the road, general affluence, and, not least, religion-backed moral teaching—so expanded the idea of aiding strangers in distress that giving with no expectation of return became almost the norm. Almost the norm? By the twentieth century, it *is* the norm—at least, under certain circumstances. For example, when a natural disaster strikes anywhere in the world, response from governments, non-government charities, corporations, and individuals is immediate. Such outpourings of generosity were inconceivable in the past. The northern parts of China during the Han Dynasty (206 BCE–220 CE) suffered periodic earthquakes in which hundreds of thousands died. Would Rome have considered sending blankets over the Silk Road? No way, not even if this could be done expeditiously! Commiseration itself would not have crossed Rome's mind.[3] Other signs of progress in modern times include the detestation of cruelty, and, in particular, cruelty to children and animals, the unacceptability of taunting the physically deformed, and thence the unacceptability of regarding people who look different as somehow inferior.

Now, what about the other side of the ledger—the regrettable additions and losses that constitute regress? One undesirable addition is worldliness, the greed for material goods and ever higher socioeconomic status that, with the decline of an accepted social hierarchy and the loss of spiritual values, fill the emptiness at the core of our being. As for the losses, they include the virtues of physical courage, loyalty, caring, chastity, and chivalry.

Physical courage is, of course, still very much in evidence today on the battlefield and in people fighting crime, fire, natural disasters, and such like, but it is less common in the general population. Certainly less common is a stoical attitude toward life. Just think of the pills that clutter our medicine cabinet to forestall every pain and the insurance policies that protect us financially against every misfortune. Loyalty lies at the foundation of feudal society. In modern capitalist society, the idea sounds quaint as we switch from job to job for higher pay and the corner office. Caring suffers in capitalist society when nursing the sick, once a quasi-religious calling, is reduced to a contractual relationship between provider and client. Chastity is the ideal of making a total gift of oneself to the beloved as against satisfying every genital itch. Ironically, replacing chastity with self-indulgence has the effect of diminishing sexual pleasure itself. Modern libertines might envy their stiff Victorian forebears, who could be aroused by an uncovered piano leg! And then there is chivalry. I find its loss particularly sad. Chivalry has ties to religion and romance, which add a color and vividness to life that is missing in today's world. During the Middle Ages, a twelve-year-old page, who aspires to knighthood, submits to a long night's vigil, in the course of which he vows to fight only in defense of the weak. That sense of serious purpose, that commitment to manly virtue, is inconceivable in a twelve-year-old video-game champion of our time.

The pleasures and virtues of the past are not, however, forgotten. At the individual level, even as I enjoy mature sexuality, I haven't forgotten the child-hood joy of sinking my teeth into a succulent hot dog. To the contrary, I feel nostalgic toward life's simpler but still shuddering pleasures. Much the same can be said of society. Contemporary society, while embracing its own values, does not renounce old ones altogether: note the undiminished popularity, in children's books and Hollywood movies, of wise kings and beautiful queens, knights in shining armor rescuing damsels in distress, a sense of honor that unhesitatingly puts honor above life, loyalty between lord and vassal, acts of superhuman courage, and even chastity, at least as exhibited by Ingrid Berg-man (1915–1982) and her fellow nuns in the film, *Bells of St. Mary's* (1945).

CHAPTER 18

Individual Destiny: A Fantasy

I
NOW TURN TO A FANTASY of of Christian origin that bears
on individual human destiny. Why this fantasy and not some
other? It could be that I favor the Christian fantasy simply
because it happened to have made a deep impression on me when I was a child.
As an adult, I explored other religions and found Buddhism the most sympathetic, above all, in the way it filled a glaring lacuna—the absence of concern
for animals—in Christian ethics. Still, I exclude Buddhism because it sees the
human individual as a bundle of illusions and, in a sense, as non-existent. Dia-
metrically opposed is Christianity's view, which sees the human individual as a
concrete particular, with the destiny of becoming even more so in another life.
A paradox of Christianity is that, for all its emphasis on selflessness and humility and for all its realism in seeing the human individual as but dust, it elevates
us to a level that is only a little lower than angels.

SELF-CONFIDENCE: RELIGIOUS SOURCES

Only a little lower than angels? Shouldn't that give us all a measure
of self-confidence? And that's not by any means the only reassurance the *Bible*
and Christianity offer. Another, even more approbatory, is the idea that we are
all made in God's image. Yes, but I am still just one human being among many,
a circumstance that can make me feel insignificant. At this point, the parable of
the lost sheep (Luke 15: 4–7) should reassure me. In that parable, the shepherd
risks leaving ninety-nine sheep unguarded in order to find the one that has
strayed. Moreover, there is the Christian belief, never quite made official, that
every human being is a separate, divine creation. As such I can hardly be overlooked. Is low social status a heavy burden? It shouldn't be when Jesus clearly
preferred the company of the socially marginalized and disenfranchised to that
of the rich and powerful. And he did so because, in his eyes, they were more
likely to find bliss. Finally, how can one feel inferior when the Son of God has
plainly said to his followers, "Henceforth I call you not servants; for the servant

knoweth not what his lord doeth: but I have called you friends; for all things that I have heard of my Father I have made known unto you" (John 15: 15).

When friends meet, they embrace, shake hands, or raise their clasped hands in greeting. One does not kneel. Kneeling is demanded by despots. It is the homage that a subject pays his sovereign, a creature before his god. Christianity's radicalism blazes forth in the perfectionist ethics of the Sermon on the Mount (Matthew 5–7). This is widely acknowledged. Less widely acknowledged but as radical in its own way is the kneeling of the incarnate God before man. When Jesus bent low to wash Peter's feet, the disciple was shocked (John 13: 4–10). How could he not be, so contrary was that act from any recorded in the Jewish tradition or, for that matter, in any other religious tradition? In any case, Jesus's unprecedented gesture, coming on top of the hints of human exceptionalism in the Old Testament, so dramatically elevates the human individual that Christianity at its most imaginative sees everyone as royal.[1] For example, at a certain point in the wedding ceremony of the Orthodox Church, a crown is held over the head of the groom and another over the head of the bride. The two may be yokels in the eyes of the world, but, in the eyes of the Orthodox Church, they are king and queen.

This attitude and the practice that goes along with it are not just confined within the walls of a church. They have filtered into the larger society and even into glittering worldly courts. Allow me to bring up again Louis XIV. The Sun King is power absolute, yet, when he encounters a maid in the corridor, he removes his hat out of respect for an equal in the eyes of God. I might also bring up Oscar Wilde—a worldly man who enjoys the company of aristocrats among whom he dispenses his gifts of wit. Yet his ideal society is socialist and democratic. He imagines it, however, to be one in which not just everyone is equal—"How boring!" he might say—but everyone is an aristocrat, with all the eccentricities of that class.[2]

That these examples can seem odd shows how far the West has forgotten the religious root of its ideals. Does the ideal of equality exist in comparable degree in other civilizations? I know of none in which a king feels obliged to bow to the maid and a noble lady is duty-bound to thank the footman who has just performed a service.[3] But Confucianist China does offer something similar. To Confucians, society is a courtly dance in which, though not everyone is noble, everyone, as participant in the dance, is fully deserving of respect.[4]

SELF-CONFIDENCE: SECULAR SOURCES

Christianity elevates the individual, as does Confucianism, though not quite so openly. Nevertheless, the effectiveness of these belief systems to empower the individual in society is extremely limited. All too common the person handicapped by poverty or minority status, so often the target of contumely, lacks self-confidence and self-esteem. What can be done? In regard to the poor, enlightened society's strategy is to provide them with the educational and economic means to rise out of poverty and join the middle class. With proper planning, it can work. In regard to minority persons, enlightened society's strategy is the same, but, when that doesn't work with hoped-for speed, it urges that they find self-confidence in their own culture and language. Strength and a sense of self, they argue, lie in belonging firmly to a group. This is true, but it is only unambiguously true when the group to which one belongs is isolated and protected against all other groups whose achievements and values might challenge its own. That degree of isolation doesn't exist in today's interconnected world, and it was rare even in the past—at least during the past century or so. What, then, is the alternative?

One alternative is to inculcate, beginning in childhood, the doctrine that everyone is a cosmopolite, a citizen of the world. Now, this isn't a modern idea—a model of society dreamed up by an ivory-tower political scientist. It was, in fact, how primitive peoples saw their world and themselves. Their self-confidence lay in the belief—a mistaken one, it turned out—that they were the only humans on Earth, that their culture was a world culture. Ethnic minorities can never have that kind of self-confidence, and, however loud and often they declare pride in their culture, they know very well that its superiority is far from being recognized by their powerful neighbors, except in subtly patronizing ways. Let me repeat: whereas the Inuit during the early twentieth century could still believe that white men came to them to seek knowledge and wisdom, ethnic minorities of our day can hardly believe that tourists come to them for any other reason than pot stickers and hot tamale.

On racial sensitivity society has changed dramatically for the better. Even a-half century or so ago, middle-class white Americans did not hesitate to describe periodic visits to ethnic neighborhoods as "slumming," at least among themselves. Today, they would not use that word, would indeed eschew the very thought. Today, their efforts are more likely to be directed at preserving and promoting ethnic ways of life, which they do in the name of cultural diversity—the liberal mantra of our time. As for the ethnic leaders, they no longer see their neighborhoods as ghettos in which people of limited opportunity and means are constrained to live. It is now the fashion to regard such places as rich in culture and social history, places to be proud of.

Much of this new appraisal is no doubt genuine. There is, however, a dark side to it; namely, the desire on the part of ethnic leaders to retain their base of political power. To do so, their people must be homogeneous, needy, of one culture, and not too inclined to venture forth into the larger world. But how can this be done? Children, by going to school, do venture into the larger world. They grow up struggling to learn arithmetic and science and, back home, customary beliefs and practices. Torn between two ways of thinking, two sets of values, and two loyalties, they can lose confidence, a sense of who they are and who they ought to be.

The cosmopolitan alternative takes a radically different approach. It doesn't split culture and knowledge into "ours" and "theirs"; rather, it starts with the assumption that every child is, by right, the inheritor of the best that humans, both in the past and in the present, have to offer.[6] By what right? The right of a being made in the image of God, "crowned with glory and honor" (Psalm 8: 5) and endowed with the remarkable senses and mind that I expatiated on. A child's intellectual horizon may be limited by necessity to the culture in which he or she is raised, but to insist that this be so as a matter of pride is wrong.

Allow me to bring up again my own childhood. In a one-room school in war-ravage China, I rubbed shoulders with the great minds and heroes of the world, past and present: Isaac Newton, Benjamin Franklin, James Watts, and others. It never occurred to me that they might not be Chinese. I—and I am sure the other Chinese children, too—knew them simply as admirable individuals, whose ingenuity, knowledge, courage, or piety we wanted to emulate. Their company at an impressionable stage of our life gave us self-confidence, a feeling that, even if we didn't belong to the ranks of the great, we were rightfully there as their cup-bearers. We saw ourselves as an integral part of this exciting, large, and expanding world. The result was a sense of possibility that served us well in later years as we confronted harsh realities, including world war and our own limitations.

When affluent white Americans urge ethnics to preserve their way of life, I grow suspicious, for I do not see them practicing what they preach. They may cultivate a sentimental regard for the cooking, clothing, language, music, and dance of their German, Polish, Norwegian, or Irish forebears, but this doesn't in the least prevent them from devoting the greater part of their effort studying mathematics and physics and taking on, additionally, the *Bhagavad-Gita* (c. 400 BCE–c. 400 CE) or the *Tao Te Ching* (c. 500 BCE): in other words, the best that world culture (civilization) has to offer. Those who insist that traditional or ethnic culture be made the basis of a people's self-esteem do have, of course, a point, for there is little doubt that both are more easily acquired there. All too often forgotten, however, is that all cultures have weaknesses, the most obvious of which is that they necessarily confine. In today's highly interconnected world, it is implausible that people anywhere will not know, if only dimly, that they may have missed opportunities to achieve the most they are capable of in their one-and-only time on Earth. To avoid making a fetish of culture, to prevent it from being more a prison than a base for growth, we need to bear in mind the following facts.

One: a culture worthy of the name is a living entity, changing over the years as it picks up influences from other peoples and places. If it has to be strenuously preserved, it can hardly be said to be living, and to insist, nevertheless, that people stay in it amounts to incarceration.

Two: cultures are not the frail flowers that some preservation-minded people think. They have surprisingly deep roots. At an international conference on nanotechnology, scientists from all over the world may use English as their common language, and they even dress much alike. Yet this hardly means they have lost their culture. One can still tell apart a Chinese from a Japanese, a Swede from a Dane, or, to the sharp-eyed, even a Castilian from a Catalonian. Moreover, operating successfully on the world stage gives these scientists supreme confidence, which makes them more—not less—proud of the roots that have nurtured them.[7]

Three: in any culture, there are beliefs and practices that are unworthy of being continued and should be retained only in the history books as a matter of record. Think of foot-binding in China. Are the Chinese less Chinese because they have given up a practice of many centuries? Think of India's caste system. Its abandonment substantially alters an ancient tradition, but educated Indians, with their eyes on a more just and prosperous future, do not in the least mind.

Four: in any lively folkway there may well be certain beliefs, practices, artworks, and moral standards that contribute to the human (as distinct from merely a particular group's) sense of self. These rightly belong to world culture. Why isn't more attention drawn to them rather than to the exotica and esoterica that swell tourist shops and ethnic-cultural festivals?

Five: a human individual's ability to see the subtlety and scope of the real far exceeds the necessarily standardized knowledge and practice of his group. An anthropologist venturing into a culture noted for its strange ways and fearful that communication with locals might be difficult may be pleasantly surprised to find someone much like him in his willingness to explore beyond his own cultural belt-line.[8]

VARIETY: THE GROUP VS. THE INDIVIDUAL

Valuing the group above the individual is grounded in the biological calculus of survival. Academics, however, have in their own way contributed to this partiality for the group. Consider biologists and social scientists. When a species of plant or animal is threatened or dies out, biologists feel—as increasingly non-biologists also feel—a sense of loss. They don't mourn the withering of one plant or the death of one animal, unless it is endowed with human characteristics, as a pet plant or animal can be. Social scientists are the same. Their concern is with the group, not the individual. When they speak of human variety, they have in mind the variety of peoples and cultures in the world, not individual differences. By contrast, humanists make a point of studying the individual—the important man or woman, naturally, but not exclusively—for it is their understanding that every human being has a unique take on reality and counts, if only for that reason.

People and culture also count. Their decline and possible extinction rightly cause concern. Two points need to be made about them, however. One is that, even as a culture dies, the people who once sustained it may not only live, but flourish under a different culture. This possibility cheers humanists, for their natural sympathy is more with human beings—their survival and growth— than with the permanence of a particular way of life. On the other hand, some humanists are also cultural historians, in which case they have a stake in seeing to it that material culture and languages do not disappear.

This brings me to my second point, which is that cultures and languages need not disappear irretrievably, for so long as tokens remain we know how to resurrect pieces of the past—rebuild a Viking ship, a Romanesque church, or a Shinto shrine. As for language, a few on the point of distinction such as Welsh have been successfully revived. Moreover, not just particular objects, but entire landscapes and scenarios from even the distant past might be given a fleeting new life. How is it that we—especially in academia—don't grasp this commonplace fact?[9] Perhaps because we snobbishly disdain movies. We fail to see that the movie industry at its best has managed to recreate in admirable detail everything from Rome under Commodus to the Irish Boston of the 1900s, with dress correct down to the last fold of the toga or the last button on the waistcoat and with actors speaking Latin or Irish brogue, as the period and place demand. True, these scenarios, absent the hum of daily life, have a dream-like quality, but what reconstructions of the past don't? Are the densely footnoted works of learned historians more real?

Individual human beings are another story. When a woman dies, she carries away with her forever a way of seeing and experiencing. In this sense, the death of a human individual is like the extinction of an entire plant or animal species. The claim may sound exaggerated. What, after all, is the worth of a human individual's experience? Granted that it is unique, but it can still be of a trivial kind. Most of us, for all our bias in favor of our fellow humans, probably think the extinction of the dodo a greater loss than the death of the grocer next door: a species's way of life is unique to a degree that cannot be said of the way of life of an ordinary human being. What, after all, is so special about our life?

TRUTH AND FREE WILL

My experiences are mostly banal. The few exceptions are those that touch on beauty, love, and truth. They are the only things of value in my life and no doubt also in the lives of other people. Beauty, love, and truth are, however, high abstractions. Hardly any two persons have the same experiences in mind when they use them. If I nevertheless use them, it is because I see them—these abstract nouns, these Platonic ideal forms—as disguised adjectives, charged qualities that can draw us up to higher states of being. Plato specifically attributes such power to beauty, but, if beauty, why not also love? Christianity sees love rather than beauty as the primary lure. Both lures, for all their power to move us, remain highly abstract, but their abstractness may be an advantage in that it discourages us from thinking that we can ever reach their highest manifestation. Attainable are the specific events and experiences that we encounter on the way up, and these we ought to embrace without being permanently seduced.

What about truth? Both Platonism and Christianity privilege truth. Capacity for impersonal truth is the divine spark in us. The capacity may be there, but it is rarely exercised. Of course, people want to know why certain things happen that disrupt the norm of life, such as a flood or drought, or even about the social norm itself when it runs counter to intuitions of fairness. Many explanations are offered but more to soothe anxiety and to prepare one how to cope than out of a desire for truth. An exception would seem to be the stars. Knowledge of them has obvious practical use, such as aligning city walls and navigation. In Western civilization, however, it has gone much further to that which cannot be seen; namely, the laws that subtend stellar motion.

Astronomy has always been a glamorous science: the very image of a human being alone on a high mountain top, peering through a giant telescope at the distant stars and galaxies, gives one an air of otherworldliness that inspires. Society was and is willing to spend enormous fortunes for a kind of knowledge that has no conceivable application. Not only the bright and learned, but people in ordinary walks of life want to know. For their part, scientists such as Stephen Hawking (b. 1942), Freeman Dyson (b. 1923), and Martin Rees (b. 1942) are willing to oblige, as though keeping the knowledge to themselves is morally reprehensible.[10]

Besides truths about nature are truths about society and human psychology. These, too, are buried, but finding them and bringing them to light is not limited to the bright and learned. The "pure of heart" also can. Common lore has it that an innocent child, not a wise counselor, sees that the emperor has no clothes; a wise fool, not a worldly sophisticate, sees the tawdry reality behind the social facade, the insecurity behind the boastfulness.

Truth, I have suggested, outranks even love and a sense of beauty, as we ordinarily understand these words. It does so by preventing the one from becoming sentimental and the other from becoming shallow. To the extent that our love is sentimental and our sense of beauty shallow, we are not quite real. When I say that my experiences in life don't amount to much, even though in sum they are one of a kind, I am referring to these deficiencies—to the fact that I am more shadow play than substance. And the same applies more or less to other people. What is the cure? Truth. Its power lies in revealing the falsities in us, a process that can be stressful. In the opposite direction, its power lies in revealing hitherto unrecognized capabilities—for example, turning human love (*eros*) into divine love (*philia*)—but that process, too, can be stressful. Who, then, will respond to the lures—and respond with what could seem unerring appropriateness? The answer, in a phrase, is "the pure in heart."

But, if God is just, why are few of us pure in heart? This stark fact forces me to return to the problem of inequality. Bad as the socioeconomic inequalities are, as bad and more resistant to correction are those of the heart: some people are just more open and receptive and, therefore, more perceptive than are others. The star-studded night sky and the dew-studded leaf are there for all to admire, yet few appreciate the splendor of the one and the charm of the other. Great teachers cast their message to the multitude, all presumably sound of hearing, yet only a few truly hear. There is ample appeal in almost any natural environment and much, too, in built environments. Still, while many look, only a few see. All too often we move through the beauties of creation like cockroaches scuttling across the floor of a symphony hall, blind to its architecture and deaf to its music.

As for the source of human perceptual obtuseness, it may lie more in defects of the will than in defects of the senses and mind. Our will, which we believe to be free, enables us to choose, but we often choose wrongly, our judgments biased by our frailties, sins, prejudices, and the external circumstances of life. The pure in heart are also unfree, and their will is also biased—but by "the grace of God." The grace of God—or something equally mysterious—gives them a disposition, a quality of attentiveness, that enables them to be unusually open to truth, beauty, and the good. Do we wish to be pure in heart? Not really, not if we have to give up the illusions of choice and agency, of being the master of our fate. A bloated egoism, unrecognized by the impure in heart, is the nature of the disease. So here, then, is one inequality that resists correction. It will still be there when gross socioeconomic inequalities have been removed.

If it is hard to hear the Gospel say, "because they seeing see not; and hearing they hear not, neither do they understand" (Matthew 13: 13), it is even harder to hear, "That unto every one which hath shall be given; and from him that hath not, even that he hath shall be taken away from him" (Luke 19: 26). What can be more unjust? The unjustness of the saying somewhat diminishes if we, again, see how will or free will plays out in life. Free will, when considered as that quality of attentiveness motivated by a longing for the Good and exercised in daily tasks and encounters, leads to new opportunities for engagement with reality, acting on which leads to still more opportunities. In contrast, those who misuse their will, which in practice almost always means obstinacy in the service of self-aggrandizement, are blinkered by the effort and, with the narrowing and channeling of their vision, lose whatever capacity they have to recognize the opportunities that lie along their paths.

LONGING FOR THE LOSS OF SELF

In the face of excessive individualism and fragmentation, which is a feature of modern life, and in the face of a consciousness that is vexed by questions of self and free will, truth and falsehood, right and wrong, goodness and evil, there is an understandable desire to be rid of them. Of the many ways available, the most common is to submit ourselves to the beliefs and settled opinions of a larger whole: the group or community. We submit willingly and unthinkingly. Once in a while, however, we may pause to ask, "What is a good community and even a perfect community?" For, if one must lose the self in a larger whole, we prefer that larger whole be perfect. One definition of the perfect community is that its members interact with no miscues and misunderstandings. Examples include the atomic nucleus and its ring of electrons, the sun and its planets, and the north star around which other stars rotate. Plant communities, in the complex relationships of their constituent parts, are necessarily less perfect, animal communities even less so, and human communities least of all.[11]

In an imperfect community, individual contends with individual, group with group. Dictators have always had a low tolerance for contentions. They strive for maximum harmony in their world, using the orderly motion of the stars as a model. Democracy cannot wish for total harmony even as an ideal: it promotes individuality and has to be satisfied with a measure of chaos. Under dictatorships people resent being reduced to obedient matter. Under democracies they suffer in the opposite direction: too much freedom, disorientation, and isolation even in the midst of milling crowd. Under either regime humans are dissatisfied—a dissatisfaction that derives, ultimately, from their ability to think and reflect. What are the solutions? There are a number of them: chemical, as in alcohol and drugs; personal, as in suicide; social, as in losing the self in a tight-knit community, in a modern organization that promises busyness, or in a fascist state that smothers all individuality. At the most exalted level there is the mystical, religious solution of erasing the self in Brahman, Nirvana, Oceanic Oneness.

INDIVIDUALITY AS A CHRISTIAN IDEAL

In sharp opposition to the ideal of self-loss in Asian religions is the Christian ideal of self-gain. Gain in what? Gain in individuality and perfection that does not even end with death, for the resurrected body continues to develop until it reaches a state intended by God from the beginning.

I now indulge in a fantasy of Christian inspiration, the merit of which is that it allows me to imagine playfully certain necessary differences between life in heaven and even exemplary life on Earth. In heaven, the saints relish solitude: it is when they recollect the self and, so recollected, are enabled to commune with God in deep intimacy. They also relish conversation with each other. Their very individuality means they have unique experiences and insights to share. On Earth, individuality, far from being an advantage to communication, can actually be a hindrance. Awareness of one's own uniqueness and that of one's potential conversational partner makes them both self-conscious and wary, so much so that an exchange of views may not even begin. Once begun, misunderstandings and disagreements surface that may have little to do with the difficulty of a topic or with the logical irreconcilability of different viewpoints; rather they lie in egotism: both partners are too enamored of their respective self to listen truly to the other. Real exchange of ideas is as much a game of love as an intellectual tryst. Needless to say, there is no lack of love or intelligence in heaven.

Saints, presumably, also spend much time in groups, as we do on Earth. Unlike us, however, they don't meet to discuss the extension of municipal sewers or to petition God for more sunshine. They don't form communities either, at least not those of "work, toil, and tribulation" that Martin Buber (1878–1965) considered "true." Heaven simply hasn't the survival needs and hostile forces that bind people together. What heaven does have may resemble the best freely formed societies in the developed world. Saints congregate, as the fortunate on Earth do, for the pure pleasure of one another's company and for certain common undertakings, such as enhancing knowledge and making joyful sounds—music—in praise of God.

REALITY AND THE IDEA OF PERFECTION

At this point, the image of heavenly choirs in white gowns returns. This is embarrassing, for, when we envisage saints in heaven, we ought to see figures of enormous heft—like mountains—and not figures that have less substance than we do. As for us, we are solid only in the sense that we have body and mass; spiritually and psychologically, we are "insubstantial dreams." Is there a way, then, to address the impasse? I believe there is, one that reaches back to St. Anselm of Canterbury (1033–1109) and is taken up again by René Descartes (1596–1650). It is a way of thinking that links the perfect with the real or, as they would say, with existence.

Whatever is perfect has to exist—existence or reality being part of perfection's meaning. An argument that was originally designed to prove the existence of God can be modified to illuminate the status of human beings. One modification is to focus on the idea that perfection comes in degrees and that, the more perfect a being is, the greater is its reality. We humans are flawed creatures and on that account shadowy, not quite real. Saints in heaven, by comparison, have a solidity—a realness—that we earthly beings can barely imagine. To the extent that we are able to come closer to perfection, we become ipso facto more real. There is no postponement, no rest, however. Even in this life, we are admonished to be perfect (Matthew 5: 48), which is to say, real.

The demand makes us uneasy, for we know it cannot be met without pain. The old saying that one is made "perfect through sufferings" (Hebrews 2: 10) has the ring of truth. On Earth we are exposed to the brute forces of nature and society, which no one—and certainly not the good—can avoid. We also suffer from being agents who act on the world, and that necessarily means overcoming some sort of barrier. This is true even in art: the Carrara marble block resists being turned into Michaelangelo's divine "David," and the virgin paper resists being made to carry "Ode to a Nightingale" (1819), the famous poem by John Keats (1795–1821). Saints in heaven are free from natural and social shocks, and no doubt they don't have to strain their muscles to put up buildings; but, to the extent that they are creative agents—indeed, much more creative than we are—they must overcome a pre-existent state, and that means effort and stress.

A deeper source of stress that is perfection—moral perfection—involves an unresolved and, it would seem, unresolvable contradiction. A good person is expected to have more substance than most of us have, to be more solidly present in the world than most of us are. And that can only mean that he or she is also more visible. In addition, the good man or woman is expected to be self-less, without an obtrusive ego, and hence should be less visible than people who like to strut. In biblical language, a Christian is urged to be a light to the world (John 8: 12), a lamp that is put on a lamp-stand and not under the meal-tub. In addition, he or she is also urged to pray in secret, not to let the left hand know the good that the right hand has done, not to attract attention and praise to oneself. The contradiction can be expected to be even more glaring in heaven, for, unlike us, the saints are fully achieved—solid and bright as burnished steel. How, then, are they to make themselves inconspicuous?

By now it should be clear why I am partial to this Christian fantasy. It provides a dual grounding for what I consider to be important in life: one is to go through it without becoming a cheap print of society's fads and abominations; and the other, more positive, is to be an authentic individual—which, to me, means to be good and (thus) a real and (thus) a tangible presence yet one that, in the absence of a bloated ego, is easily overlooked. At this juncture, I see a convergence of Buddhist and Christian views. In both, moral perfection entails a paradox: whereas Buddhism postulates a self whose aim is to be a non-self, Christianity postulates a self—a real and highly individuated being—who strives to be self-less.

HUMANISM AND RELIGION

Humanism in its modern form emerged with the recovery of classical learning. Studying the classics led men of the Renaissance to appreciate the remarkable achievements of antiquity and to an enlarged view of what it is to be human. This pagan boost, added to that given by Christianity, made Renaissance men proud. In time, however, humanism in Europe sought to distance itself from religion. To the extent that this meant discarding superstitious beliefs and practices, people continued to gain freedom and stature. To the extent that this meant discarding, one by one, all supra-natural notions of human nature and destiny, people suffered diminishment. Ironically, secularism and science, forces that were originally harnessed to elevate human dignity, end by reducing a creature supposedly made in God's image either to an animal that is only a little higher than the ape or to a socioeconomic abstraction and statistic.

To secular-scientific humanists, the ultimate and inescapable constraint in life is death. Only a corpse remains, and that soon turns into dust. Despite these stark facts, humanists lead their lives no less cheerfully than do those of religious faith. It may be that a residual credence in human worth and destiny, derived from religion, lingers unrecognized in their minds. Devoting themselves to good causes—social justice, literacy, animal rights, bioethics, ecological democracy, and so on—is also an effective means of forgetting. In a real sense, good causes are their opium. And may they continue to be addictive and numbing, for it is hard to imagine what the world will be like when those of good will, but ungrounded in any religious belief or metaphysical intuition, begin to question the basis of their secular faith and wake up to the full, bitter understanding of the ultimate futility of their effort.[13]

PART VI

Parting Thoughts

CHAPTER 19

Becoming Whole

———————————

THROUGHOUT THIS BOOK I have introduced stories from Buddhism and Christianity. Both faiths presuppose life continuing beyond death, thus allowing for further change and growth or—in religious language—opportunities to redeem oneself. These stories appeal to me not from fear of death. Truth to tell, like all insomniacs tortured by wakefulness, I yearn for release and oblivion. No, these stories appeal to me because they address my craving for some sort of eventual justice. Even as a child I was uncomfortably aware of how greatly human fate differed. This awareness increased and became more vexatious as I knew more about the world. Images of the extremes haunt me in all their vivid specificity: a cantilevered house on Big Sur overlooking the Pacific Ocean, juxtaposed against a slum shack in Lagos; a teenager expounding the Q-binomial theorem to his bright classmates, juxtaposed against a victim of Down's syndrome drooling at the mouth; a dying Hubert Humphrey (1911–1978), ripe in years and achievements, surrounded by relatives, friends, doctors, and nurses, juxtaposed against a child in Darfur dying of starvation in a refugee camp.

In a way, I came to see that, at least in the developed world, certain inequalities diminish, if the focus is on the quality of experience rather than on the quality and quantity of goods and landed properties. To own legally is not at all the same thing as to possess. One can have the beauty of art and nature only when one is in the right state of mind. If the good inherit Earth, it is because they have the right state of mind—they look and see, hear and understand. Most of us do not qualify as good; most of us are too blinded by ambition, envy, greed, and vanity to have what we own. Ironically, sins contribute to justice by handicapping the talented and beautiful and, above all, the powerful and rich.

Still, I remain bothered, not satisfied with these consoling answers. They don't resolve the extreme differences in fate that I noted above. The only course that I find satisfactory and just is for the moment of death to be the beginning rather than the end. Both Christianity and Buddhism offer a new beginning. Although I am under Christianity's spell, I nevertheless find a key Buddhist doctrine of the afterlife more imaginatively rewarding. To the Buddhist, death leads to another incarnation. Scientists may find the idea risible as, I have to admit, I do myself, yet there is something to like about it: it enables one to imagine an afterlife concretely, not as a saint in a white robe but as, say, a toad, then a horse, and then, after aeons of lives, a wise and kindly chimpanzee.

The special merit of the Buddhist story is that it teaches one to be patient infinitely and to realize that one's karma is affected by even the slightest impulse to vanity or envy, the smallest act of unkindness or inconsideration, as it is affected, in the other direction, by the slightest tug of compassion and the smallest act of helpfulness. Seen in this light, a toad's opportunities for improvement must be extremely limited and those of a horse not much more. We humans, by comparison, have more opportunities and can make better use of them. Yet, if we are honest with ourselves, what real progress do we make in things that matter even in a long life? What progress have I made in four-score years of existence?

In matters of the mind, with the passing of years I obviously know more. I estimate that I've read thousands of books in a lifetime, but how pitifully small this number is compared with the 8,000,000 in my university's library! More to the point is whether the more I know with age matters, even to me. Maybe that doubt is itself evidence of an improvement, for it clearly wasn't entertained by me in brazen youth. In morals? In what sense am I a better person now than I was, say, seventy years ago, when I was ten? In one sense: the more I know how vulgar (i.e., common) evil is, the less I am tempted by it. A sort of moral snobbery guards me against elevating myself at another's expense, which is the form of evil most available to me. Can this be counted as a moral improvement? Perhaps, but how limited and ambiguous!

Only in self-knowledge can I say that I have made read progress. Part of it is simply biological maturation. Thus, at the verge of puberty, sexual stirrings made me see two areas of darkness in my future: one, the impossibility of experiencing reciprocated love and, the other, the inevitability of death. The first casts a pall of sadness and guilt in my deepest affections, the second a nagging premonition of disaster even when the sun shines and the birds sing. Self-knowledge doesn't just come with biological maturation; it can intrude anytime, at any stage of life. Thus, at age twelve, in Australia, I was much taken with the story of Jesus, even though I didn't know what to make of the miracles. At age twenty-three, in California's Death Valley, I was to discover the desert as my objective correlative, my psychic self made visible in a stark, mineral landscape. Self-knowledge is also a result of effort, though the initial stimulus for starting the effort can remain mysterious. Thus, at age seventy-four, in Madison, Wisconsin, I began to listen to J. S. Bach attentively, deriving from his works, first, the pleasure of recognizing a theme, then the thrill of being lifted to a sublime world, and, finally, the reassurance and comfort of having found a true home. Until I made the effort, I couldn't possibly know that the unease at my psychic core could find balm in the works of a Leipzig Kappelmeister.

Progress is a recurrent theme in this book, as is also the idea of an individual making his or her journey through life. The notion that what matters is the journey, not the final destination, has never had much appeal, for I can't see the point of embarking on a journey unless something desirable awaits me at the end. I am still prone to see life as directional and having a purpose, and so I shall return to these considerations in my concluding remarks. But, before I do so, I need to make a correction. A problem with too much emphasis on progress is its tendency to devalue the intervening stages. Thus, I might see dinosaurs as existing only so that human beings can emerge and childhood as merely a step toward adulthood. Recognizing that each stage in an individual's growth has its own perfection and that the myriad life-forms on planet Earth are simply different rather than different qualitatively in the upward path of evolution makes me more fully aware of nature's richness and equality.

But, then, two considerations jolt me back to progress and inequality. One is that it is evasive to say that things are simply different. After all, differences can be large or small. An *order* of difference exists between an oak leaf and an oak tree, whereas only a trivial one exists between two leaves on the same tree. Another example: a lion is a vastly more complex organism than the ticks that infest it, and so it is truer to say that lion and tick are incompatible and unequal rather than that they are simply different. As for the stages of growth, while it may be right to say that each stage has its own perfection, the saying is misleading in that it slights the idea of maturity—the idea that the young finds self-realization (its *telos*) in adulthood. This point takes me to the second consideration, namely, the unique path of human development. An acorn turns into an oak, a kitten turns into a cat. These are biological stories. With human beings, a cultural story runs parallel with the biological one. Biologically, some people are better endowed than others. These differences are hard to surmount and are, to me, grossly inequitable, yet they can be at least partially surmounted with the aid of cultural-educational resources. Unfortunately, the resources of society are even more unevenly distributed than are nature's gifts. The result is that the vast majority of human beings die with only a sketch of their human potential fulfilled.

A source of religion's appeal to me is that it provides some sort of salve to my need for equity. Whatever hardships a disadvantage group suffers, it can always hope that its descendants will find compensation and justice. Not so, obviously, for the individual member—unless there is life beyond death. Buddhism postulates that death is not the end: a being can work out its salvation through successive incarnations. A corollary of the belief in incarnations is that the emaciated cow, the shaggy dog, or indeed any other animal could be me in a previous embodiment. From Buddhism I learn to show respect for nonhuman creatures. In the end, however, Buddhism is not suited to my temperament. It doesn't promise progress in the afterlife: a being may rise from frog to chimpanzee, only to fall back to froghood. An even greater stumbling block for me is the Buddhist doctrine that, if, after aeons of time, I finally arrive at salvation, it is only to lose my individuality and merge with Oceanic Oneness.

So I am left with Christianity, a religion that, while it uniquely values human beings, also teaches that we are sinful—that is, flawed. We are indeed flawed; to this I would add that we are also, for reasons beyond our control, unfinished. Flawed and unfinished, no wonder most of us are spectral figures haunting a stage that can also seem to lack substance, not quite real. The advantage of postulating an afterlife is that it will give us the time we need to grow into what God intended us to be from the beginning—solid presences, distinctive individuals—in a place of heart-stopping beauty and vividness.

Such thoughts ought to put me on guard. Have I gone too far? Am I indulging in pure, escapist fantasy? Even my most sympathetic readers will probably think I have ventured way beyond humanist geography, however defined, to the phantasmagoria of a heated religious imagination. Yet, when I was a student at Oxford during the late 1940s, the people I admired most for their intellect and imagination would have taken the idea of an afterlife in stride. They were C. S. Lewis, J. R. R. Tolkien, Charles Williams, T. S. Eliot, W. H. Auden, Reinhold Niebuhr, Dietrich Bonhoeffer, Albert Schweitzer, Gabriel Marcel, Nikolai Berdyaev, Simone Weil, and Dorothy Day—all Christians. It is fair to say that immortality did not lure them into the Christian religion. One of them, Charles Williams (1886–1945), even declared that he could not "abide the reward." Immortality, to them, was rather a consequence (and by no means the most important consequence) of their deep understanding of, and intimate engagement with, the figure of Christ.

How the world has changed in the last fifty years! Overwhelmingly, the world today is secular/materialist, an assertion not contradicted by the rise of religious fundamentalism, which, to me, is a pathological flare in the embers of faith. In a secular/materialist world, I am an oddity. My colleagues and friends find my beliefs, insofar as they depart from the observable, incomprehensible and slightly embarrassing. For my part, I find it baffling that they do not see the need to consider the foundation of their beliefs and actions. What makes them behave the way they do in daily life, and, more to the point, what drives them to do such good deeds as saving the planet Earth or ensuring greater socioeconomic equality worldwide? Whence their sense of obligation? Is making Earth habitable for oneself, for one's children, and for one's children's children all that is needed to live happily and fulfilled? Does not the image of one generation succeeding another, each of no greater telos than handing over a few genes to the next, seem rather pointless? How modest such an image of human existence is compared with that of St. Augustine, who asked himself, "When you have learned that you are immortal—will that be enough for you?" His answer: "It will be something great, but it is too little for me."[1]

My own beliefs and actions are rooted in the teachings and stories of Christianity. I cannot say that my sympathy with the Christian religion is rational. Rather, I see it as an effect of circumstance and temperament, which is why

I have not felt compelled to spread the good news, as converts are bidden to do. Christianity presents hurdles to even the sympathetic. One is its moral extremism, as exemplified in the Sermon on the Mount. The precepts in the sermon seem to address beings of another world. They are impractical for this one. Impractical does not mean, however, unnatural or supernatural. Supernatural are the miracles, the most important of which is the resurrection of Jesus Christ (Luke 24). Resurrection postulates the existence of life beyond death. How do I see the afterlife? If I see it as a possibility, it is because immortality is part of the Christian baggage and also because, as I said at the beginning of the book, I need to see justice done but cannot see that it can be done, or even much mitigated, here on Earth. Lastly, certain facts and hints in this life encourage me to be open to something beyond death.

One such fact is the depth of evil. Does the struggle for survival, offered by the theory of biological evolution, quite explain the cruelty, the sadism, the ocean of blood that are so much a part of human history? I don't see that it does. Evil—the Force of Darkness in theological language—feels real. William James would agree. Moral life, seriously considered, is a battle that does not allow one to sit on the fence. The moral person struggles not for his own survival, but for the survival of the Good. This assertion takes me to the other pole of morality—goodness. If the depth of evil is hard to explain away, so also is the height of goodness. Superlatively good individuals, such as the beatific child, the tireless social worker, the selfless aunt, the supreme genius, hint at another order of reality. Attempts made by the biological and social sciences to account for them do not convince me, in part because I don't find the arguments persuasive, but even more because arguments are powerless against direct experience, even in passing, of human beings whose goodness makes me see them as sojourners from the kingdom of God.

At a level lower than that of supernal goodness are the aesthetic hints of another reality. Consider two of them: one auditory, the other visual. The auditory is available to the lover of music, as I am. If heaven is intimacy with God and communal adoration, then I already have a hint of it listening to J. S. Bach's *Mass in B minor* (1729), in the course of which I feel the coziness of a tête-à-tête and the glory of communion amidst throngs of saints in cathedral space. The visual is an inexpungible sense of a fuller, more splendid world elsewhere. Even on Earth our senses are equipped to give us the "lilies of the field" and other marvels of nature and art; only we seldom use them to the full, preferring to go through life as though perpetually afflicted with a head cold. When the cold lifts, our surroundings have the fresh look of a new creation; or, to use the illustration I provided in a previous chapter, we may be likened to mariners who steer through an indented coast with the help of a radar screen that is located below the deck. In time, the mariners (that is, us) come to accept the dark, claustrophobic space in the hull as the only reality. Imagine our astonishment when we emerge on deck into sunshine and confront a reality that is richly particular and achingly beautiful.

Notes

———

TO BE HUMAN

1. A somewhat different and more precise account of "The Hours of Our Lives" is given in *American Time Use Survey,* Bureau of Labor Statistics, 2010 annual averages. The hours are based on a life expectancy of 77.8 years, as against my biblical three-score and ten.

2. Raymond Williams, *Keywords: A Vocabulary of Culture and Society* (New York: Oxford University Press, 1976), 66.

3. Yi-Fu Tuan, "Home and World, Cosmopolitanism and Ethnicity," in Ian Douglas, Richard Huggett, and Mike Robinson, eds., *Companion Encyclopedia of Geography* (London: Routledge, 1996), 939–51, and "Community, Society, and the Individual," *Geographical Review,* Vol. 92, No 3 (2002): 307–18.

CHAPTER 1

1. Norman Malcolm, *Ludwig Wittgenstein: A Memoir* (London, UK: Oxford University Press, 1958), 51–52.

CHAPTER 2

1. I attended high school in the Philippines but for only six months, too brief a period to warrant a separate chapter. I can say, however, that it was in Manilla where I developed a distaste for undigested multi-culturalism and virulent nationalism.

CHAPTER 3

1. *The Holy Bible* is referenced throughout the text as the literary work it is (see Chapter 16, note 1). Hereinafter, I shorten the title to the *Bible*.

CHAPTER 5

1. See, for example, Joseph M. Marshall, III, *The Lakota Way: Stories and Lessons for Living* (New York: Viking Compass, 2001).

CHAPTER 6

1. R. J. Williams, *You Are Extraordinary* (New York: Random House, 1967), and "Nutritional Individuality," *Human Nature* (June 1978): 46–53.

2. Jacques Hadamard, *The Psychology of Invention in the Mathematical Field* (Princeton, NJ: Princeton University Press, 1949), 115.

3. M. S. Gazzaniga, *Nature's Mind: The Biological Roots of Thinking, Emotions, Sexuality, Language, and Intelligence* (New York: Basic Books, 1992).

4. Yi-Fu Tuan, "Place and Culture: Analeptic for Individuality and the World's Indifference," in Wayne Franklin and Michael Steiner, eds., *Mapping American Culture* (Iowa City: University of Iowa Press, 1992), 28–29, and Ilham Dilman, *Love and Human Separateness* (Oxford: Blackwell, 1987).

5. Jules Henry, *Jungle People: A Kaingang Tribe of the Highlands of Brazil* (New York: J. J. Augustin, 1941), 18, and Lorna Marshall, *The Kung of Nyae Nyae* (Cambridge, MA: Harvard University Press, 1976), 249.

6. Victor Zuckerkandl, *Man the Musician* (Princeton, NJ: Princeton University Press, 1973), 21.

7. David Evans, "Neighbors," from *Shenandoah* (Summer 1971): 42.

8. Michael Erard, "How Many Languages? Linguists Discover New Tongues in China," *Science*, Vol. 324 (April 17, 2009): 332–33.

9. John R. Stilgoe, "Boyhood Landscape and Repetition," in George F. Thompson, ed., *Landscape in America* (Austin: University of Texas Press, 1995), 183–202.

10. As quoted in Joseph Epstein, *Friendship: An Exposé* (Boston, MA: Houghton Mifflin, 2006), 205. The quotation is from one of Johnson's *Idler* essays.

11. Edward Relph, "Place," in Ian Douglas, Richard Huggett, and Mike Robinson, eds., *Companion Encyclopedia of Geography* (London, UK: Routledge, 1996), 906–22, and Tim Cresswell, *Place: A Short Introduction* (Oxford, UK: Blackwell, 2004).

12. Owen H. Hufton, *The Poor in Eighteenth-Century France, 1750–1789* (Oxford, UK: Clarendon Press, 1974), 360–63.

13. M. I. Finley, *The World of Strangers* (Harmondsworth, Middlesex, UK: Penguin, 1979), 64.

14. Yi-Fu Tuan, "Community and Place: A Skeptical View," in Shue Tuck Wong, ed., *Person, Place and Thing* (Baton Rouge: Louisiana State University, Geoscience and Man, No. 31, 1992), 50.

15. Peter Laslett, *The World We Have Lost* (New York: Charles Scribner's Sons, 1971), 5.

16. Karl A. Nowotny, *Beiträge zur Geschiche des Weltbildes* (Vienna, Austria: Verlag Ferdinand Berber & Söhne, 1969).

17. Archeologists are unsure as to where—possibly Asia or Meso-America.

18. Paul Wheatley, *The Pivot of the Four Quarters* (Chicago: Aldine, 1971).

19. Robert Brain, *Friends and Lovers* (New York: Basic Books, 1976), 145–64.

20. Yi-Fu Tuan, *Cosmos and Hearth* (Minneapolis: University of Minnesota Press, 1996), and "Home and World, Cosmopolitanism and Ethnicity," in Ian Douglas et. al., eds., *op. cit.,* 939–51.

CHAPTER 7

1. I have stressed the material changes demanded by greater self-awareness. There were also a number of non-material changes. For example, from the sixteenth century onward, literate people began using "I" with greater frequency in their writing, and words such as "self-love," "self-knowledge," "self-pity," "ego," "character," "melancholy," and "embarrassment" began to enter English and French literature.

2. William Shakespeare, *As You Like It*, Act II, Scene VII.

3. Yi-Fu Tuan, *Segmented Worlds and Self: Group Life and Individual Consciousness* (Minneapolis: University of Minnesota Press, 1982).

CHAPTER 8

1. Yi-Fu Tuan, "Community, Society, and the Individual," *Geographical Review*, Vol. 92, No. 3 (July 2002): 307–8.

2. Oliver Sacks, "The Autist Artist," *New York Review of Books*, Vol. 32, No. 7 (April 25, 1985): 17–21.

3. John Updike, "The City," in *Trust Me* (New York: Alfred A. Knopf, 1987), 34–53.

CHAPTER 9

1. Michael André Bernstein, "Walt Benjamin's Long, Limited View," *New Republic* (December 26, 1997): 39.

2. Protagoras, *Fragment I*. See Robert Nisbet, *History of the Idea of Progress* (New York: Basic Books, 1980), 22.

3. Carol Ziosowitz Sterns and Peter N. Stearns, *Anger: The Struggle for Emotional Control in America's History* (Chicago: University of Chicago Press, 1986).

4. From Aristotle onward, "health" and "happiness" are proper objects of desire and, so, even of envy. The same is not true of "wealth," "reputation," and "family happiness."

CHAPTER 10

1. Adolf Friedrich, "Die Forschung über das frühzeitliche jagertum," *Paideuma*, Vol. 2 (1941–1943): 21.

2. Elizabeth Kolbert, "Flesh of Your Flesh," *The New Yorker* (November 9, 2009): 74.

3. Reinaldo Arenas, *Before the Night Falls* (New York: Penguin Group, 1994) 20–21.

4. Yi-Fu Tuan, *Dominance and Affection: The Making of Pets* (New Haven, CT: Yale University Press, 1984).

5. Jean-Paul Sartre, *Saint Genet* (New York: George Braziller, 1963), 360–61.

6. Fung Yu-lan, *A Short History of Chinese Philosophy* (New York: Macmillan, 1959), 18.

7. Confucius, *Analects* 10: 11

8. Thomas E. Ricks, *Making the Corps* (New York: Charles Scribner Sons, 1997), 95.

9. Simon Leys, in the foreword to Yang Jiang, *Lost in the Crowd* (Melbourne, Australia: McPhae Gribble, 1989) 6.

10. *The New York Times* (July 22, 1999).

11. Epictetus, *Dissertationes* 4.

12. Roy Perrott, *The Aristocrats: A Portrait of Britain's Nobility and Their Way of Life Today* (London, UK: Weidenfeld and Nicolson, 1968), 202.

13. Evon Z. Vogt and Ethel M. Albert, *People of Rimrock: A Study of Values in Five Cultures* (Cambridge, MA: Harvard University Press, 1966), 26.

14. René Grousset, *The Rise and Splendour of the Chinese Empire* (Berkeley: University of California Press, 1959), 40–41.

15. *Standard Operating Procedure*, a film by Errol Morris (Sony Pictures Classics, 2008), and Jane Mayer, "The Black Sites," *The New Yorker* (August 13, 2007): 46–57.

16. A. B. Bosworth, *Alexander and the East: The Tragedy of Triumph* (Oxford, UK: Oxford University Press, 1996).

17. David Morgan, *The Mongols* (Oxford, UK: Blackwell, 1990).

18. Yi-Fu Tuan, "Our Treatment of Environment in Ideal and Actuality," *American Scientist*, Vol. 58 (May-June, 1970): 244–49.

19. Arthur F. Wright, *The Sui Dynasty* (New York: Alfred A. Knopf, 1978), 49–50.

20. Gillette Ziegler, *The Court of Versailles in the Reighn of Louis XIV* (London, UK: Allen & Enwin, 1966), 30.

21. A remarkable scholarly book that has something favorable to say about imperialism is Lewis Feuer, *Imperialism and the Anti-Imperialist Mind* (Buffalo, NY: Pomethesus Books, 1986).

22. See Rag Saner, *Living Large in Nature: A Writer's Way to Creationism* (Chicago: The Center for American Places at Columbia College Chicago, 2010).

CHAPTER 11

1. "Cortes's Account of the City of Mexico," *Old South Leaflets* (Boston, MA: Directors of the Old South Work, Vol. 12, No. 35 (n.d.), 9–10.

CHAPTER 12

1. In this regard, we owe much to the pioneering work of geographer Johannes Gabriel Granö, who proved the human ability to map space by nonvisual means, especially by smell and sound. See his now classic book, *Pure Geography* (Baltimore, MD: The Johns Hopkins University Press, in association with the Center for American Places, 1997).

2. Ashley Montagu, *Touching: The Human Significance of the Skin* (New York: Harper & Row, 1978), 8; see, also, Constance Classen, ed., *The Book of Touch* (Oxford, UK: Berg Publishers, 2005).

3. D. H. Lawrence, *Women in Love* (London: Secker, 1921; originally published in 1920 in New York City as a limited edition of 1,250 hardcover copies), 120–21.

4. "Jade" in C. A. S. Williams, *Encyclopedia of Chinese Symbolism and Art Motives* (New York: The Julian Press, 1960), 234–35.

5. Wolfram Eberhard, *A Dictionary of Chinese Symbols* (London, UK: Routledge, 1988).

6. Dorothy Lee, "View of Self in Greek Culture, *Freedom and Culture* (Englewood Cliffs, NJ: Prentice-Hall, 1959), 144.

7. Claude Lévi-Strauss, *The Raw and the Cooked* (New York: Harper & Row, 1969).

8. Jacques Barzun, *A Stroll With William James* (New York: Harper & Row, 1983), 284.

9. Carolyn Korsmeyer, ed., *The Taste Culture Reader: Experiencing Food and Drink* (Oxford, UK: Berg Publishers, 2005).

10. Robert Rivlin and Karen Gravelle, *Deciphering the Senses* (New York: Simon & Schuster, 1984), 76; Steve Van Totler and George H. Dodd, *Perfumery* (London, UK: Kapman and Hall, 1988), 47; and Edmund T. Morris, *Fragrance* (New York: Charles Scribner's Sons, 1984), 41.

11. As quoted by Howard Nemerov, *Figures of Thought* (Boston, MA: Godine, 1978), 31.

12. Rosalind Williams, *Notes on the Underground* (Cambridge, MA: The MIT Press, 1990).

13. Jason Logan, "Scents of the City," *The New York Times* (August 30, 2009): 10.

14. Alain Corbin, *The Foul and the Fragrant: Odor and the French Social Imagination* (Cambridge, MA: Harvard University Press, 1986), 22–23.

15. Jacques Gernet, *Daily Life in China on the Eve of the Mongol Invasion 1250–1276* (London, UK: Allen & Unwin, 1962), 120–21.

16. John Updike, *Self-Consciousness* (New York: Alfred A. Knopf, 1989), 233.

17. Jamie James, *The Music of the Spheres: Music, Science, and the Natural Order of the Universe* (New York: Copernicus, 1955).

18. William Shakespeare, *Merchant of Venice*, Act V, Scene I.

19. Blaise Pascal, *Pensée's* (1670), 206.

20. Birger, Ohlson, "Sound Fields and Sonic Landscapes in Rural Environments," *Fennia*, Vol. 148 (1976) 33–43, and J. Douglas Porteous and Jane F. Mastin, "Soundscape," *Journal of Architecture Planning Research*, Vol. 2 (1985): 169–86.

21. B. Raymond Fink, *Science* (24 January 1986): 319.

22. R. Murray Schafer, *The Tuning of the World* (New York: Alfred A. Knopf, 1977).

23. Julian Johnson, *Who Needs Classical Music? Cultural Choice and Musical Value* (Oxford, UK: Oxford University Press, 2002).

24. Claude Lévi-Strauss, *Myth and Meaning* (New York: Schocken Books, 1979), 18.

25. Brent Berlin and Paul Kay, *Basic Color Terms* (Berkeley: University of California Press, 1969).

26. G. K. Chesterton, *Alarms and Excursions* (New York: Dodd, Mead & Co., 1911).

27. Robert Bernard Martin, *Gerard Manley Hopkins* (New York: Putnam's, 1998), 190.

28. As quoted in Georges Poulet, *Studies in Human Time* (Baltimore, MD: The Johns Hopkins University Press, 1956), 249.

29. Yi-Fu Tuan, "Sight and Pictures," *Geographical Review*, Vol. 69, No. 4 (1979): 413–22.

30. Anaxagoras was quoted by Aristotle in *Ethica Eudemia*, 1216a. See Joseph Pieper, *Happiness and Contemplation* (London, UK: Faber & Faber, 1988), 103.

31. Dante (Durante degli Aligheri), *La Divina Commedia* (*The Inferno*), Canto 34, written between 1308–1321.

32. William Shakespeare, *The Merchant of Venice,* Act V, Scene I.

33. Aldous Huxley, "Unpainted Landscapes," *Encounter*, Vol. 19, No. 4 (1962): 41–47.

34. Helen Vendler, review of *Collected Poetry of Robinson Jeffers* (Stanford, CA: Stanford University Press, 1988), in *The New Yorker* (December 8, 1988): 98.

35. Kenneth Landscape, *Landscape Into Art* (New York: Harper & Row, 1976), 92; Simon Schama, *Landscape and Memory* (New York: Alfred A. Knopf, 1995); and Kiyohiko Munaka, *Sacred Mountains in Chinese Art* (Urbana-Champaign, IL: Krannert Art Museum, 1991).

36. Kenneth Olwig, *Landscape, Nature, and the Body Politic* (Madison: University of Wisconsin Press, 2002).

37. Georges Duby, *The Age of Cathedrals: Art and Society 980–1420* (Chicago: University of Chicago Press, 1981), 97–135, and Umberto Eco, "The Aesthetics of Light," in *Art and Beauty in the Middle Ages* (New Haven, CT: Yale University Press, 1986), 43–51.

38. Stephen Gill, *William Wordsworth: A Life* (Oxford, UK: Clarendon Press, 1989), 48–49.

39. Stanley Cavell, *The World Viewed: Reflections on the Ontology of Film* (New York: Viking Press, 1971), 23.

40. Sir John Gielgud, *Gielgud, an Actor and His Time: A Memoir* (New York: Clarkson N. Potter, 1980), 198.

41. Arthur C. Danto, *The Philosophical Disenfranchisement of Art* (New York: Columbia University Press, 1986), 96.

42. Stephen Cavell, *op. cit.*, 43.

CHAPTER 13

1. C. S. Lewis, *Letters to Malcolm* (London, UK: Fontana Books, 1966), 88.

2. James J. Y. Liu, *The Art of Chinese Poetry* (Chicago: University of Chicago Press, 1962); and Ernest Fenollosa and Ezra Pound, *The Chinese Written Character as a Medium for Poetry*, edited by Haun Saussy, Jonathan Stalling, and Lucas Klein (New York: Fordham University Press, 2008; originally published in London in 1950).

3. Isaiah Berlin, *Vico and Herder* (London, UK: Hogarth Press, 1976), 104.

4. For Galileo's image of the horse, see Italo Calvino, *Six Memos for the Next Millennium* (Cambridge, MA: Harvard University Press, 1988), 43; for Kekule's snake, see Anthony Storr, *Solitude: A Return to the Self* (New York: Free Press, 1988), 67; for Luria's slot machine, see S. E. Luria, *A Slot Machine: A Broken Test Tube: An Autobiography* (New York: Harper & Row, 1984), 75; and, on chemical metaphors, see E. Farker, "Chemical Discoveries By Means of Analogies," *Isis*, Vol. 41, Part 1 (1956), 20–26.

5. Howard Gardner, *Art, Mind, and Brain* (New York: Basic Books, 1982), 158.

6. Kenneth Grahame, *The Wind in the Willows* (New York: Heritage Press, 1944), 69–70, and Yi-Fu Tuan, "Landscape and the Making of Place: A Narrative-Descriptive Approach," *Annals of the Association of American Geographers*, Vol. 81, No. 4 (1991): 684–96.

7. Sigfried Giedion, *Architecture and the Phenomena of Transition: The Three Space Conceptions in Architecture* (Cambridge, MA: Havard University Press, 1971).

8. David Blum, "Walking to the Pavilion," *The New Yorker* (April 30, 1990): 51.

9. Iris Murdoch, interviewed by Bryan Magee in his book, *Men of Ideas: Some Creators of Contemporary Philosophy* (New York: Viking, 1979), 283.

10. Roland Barthes, *A Lover's Discourse* (New York: Hill & Wang, 1978), 167.

11. Colin M. Turnbull, "The Mbuti Pygmies: An Ethnographic Survey," *Anthropological Papers*, The American Museum of Natural History, Vol. 50, Part 3 (1965): 164.

12. Bruce Chatwin, *The Song Lines* (New York: Viking Penguin, 1987), 56 and 73, and Ronald M. Bernd and Catherine H. Bernt, *Man, Land & Myth in North Australia: The Gunwinggu People* (East Lansing: Michigan State University Press, 1970), 19 and 41.

13. John T. Ogden, "From Spatial to Aesthetic Distance in the Eighteenth Century," *Journal of the History of Ideas*, Vol. 35, No. 1 (1974): 63–78.

14. Yi-Fu Tuan, *Topophilia: A Study of Environmental Perception, Attitudes, and Values* (Englewood Cliffs, NJ: Prentice-Hall, 1974; reprinted by Columbia University Press, 1990), 129–36.

15. Thomas S. Kuhn, *The Structure of Scientific Revolution* (Chicago: University of Chicago Press, 1970), 161.

16. The term "ecology" was first coined in 1866 by the eminant German zoologist Ernst Haeckel (1834–1919).

17. James Hutton, *Theory of the Earth* (New York: Stechert-Hafner, 1959; first read before the Society of Edinburgh in 1788 and then expanded and originally published in two volumes in 1795). See, also, Stephen Toulmin and June Goodfield, *The Discovery of Time* (Chicago: University of Chicago Press, 1965), 76, and John B. Jackson, "In Search of the Proto-Landscape," in George F. Thompson, ed., *Landscape in America* (Austin: Univeristy of Texas Press, 1995), especially 48–50.

18. Edward Conze, *Buddhism: Its Essence and Development* (New York: Harper Colophon, 1975), 48–52.

19. Lucien Gallois, "Origin and Growth of Paris," *Geographical Review*, Vol. 13, No. 3 (1923): 360.

20. Alvin Schwarz, *Museum: The History of America's Treasure Houses* (New York: E. P. Dutton, 1967), 126–27.

21. John Updike, *Rabbit Redux* (New York: Fawcett Crest, 1972), 202.

22. Steven Hoelscher, *Heritage on Stage: The Invention of Ethnic Place in America's Little Switzerland* (Madison: University of Wisconsin Press, 1998).

23. Alice Calaprice, ed., *The Ultimate Quotable Einstein* (Princeton, NJ: Princeton University Press, 2011), 26.

24. Jeremy Bernstein, "Profiles: Masters of the Trade 1: Hans Albrecht Bethey," *The New Yorker* (December 3, 1979): 52.

25. Lynne White, Jr., *Machine Ex Deo* (Cambridge, MA: The MIT Press, 1968), 17.

26. On the relationship between "beauty" and "form," see Robert Adams, *Beauty in Photography: Essays in Defense of Traditional Values* (New York: Aperture, 1981), especially 21–36.

27. Subrahmanyan Chandrasekhar, *Beauty and Truth: Aesthetics and Motivations in Science* (Chicago: University of Chicago Press, 1987), 54.

28. J. R. R. Tolkien, "On Fairy-Stories," in C. S. Lewis, ed., *Essays Presented to Charles Williams* (Grand Rapids, MI: Eerdmans, 1966), 38–89, and Ann Swinfen, *In Defence of Fantasy* (London, UK: Routledge & Kegan Paul, 1984).

29. Fyodor Dostoevsky, *The Brothers Karamazov* (New York: Vintage Books, 1991; originally published as a serial in 1880 by *The Russian Messenger*), 246–64.

30. Yuhwen Wang, "The Ethical Power of Music: Ancient Greek and Chinese Thoughts," *Journal of Aesthetic Education*, Vol. 38, No.1 (2004): 89–104.

31. William James, *The Principles of Psychology, Vol. 1* (New York: Dover, 1950), 125–26.

32. Iris Murdoch, "Salvation By Words," in *Existentialists and Mystics* (New York: Allen Lane/Penguin Press, 1997), 235–42.

33. "Be Still my Soul": music by Jean Sibelius (1865–1957), from *Finlandia* (1899), and words by Katharina von Schlegel, 1752; and "When I Survey the Wondrous Cross": music anonymous but arranged by Edward Miller in 1790 and words by Isaac Watts, 1707, after Galatians 6: 14.

CHAPTER 14

1. Hans Kung, *Eternal Life? Life After Death as a Medical, Philosophical, and Theological Problem* (Garden City, NY: Doubleday, 1984).

2. Irene Masing-Delic, *Abolishing Death: A Salvation Myth of Russian Twentieth-Century Literature* (Stanford, CA: Stanford University Press, 1992).

3. Hannah Arendt, *The Human Condition* (Garden City, NY: Doubleday/Anchor, 1959), 155–223.

4. Helen Gardner, *Religion and Literature* (Oxford, UK: Oxford University Press, 1971).

5. Thomas Cahill, *The Gifts of the Jews* (New York: Anchor Books, 1998).

6. Nirvana: from the Sanskrit root *va* = "blow out" or being "blown away," "extinguished," into a state of endless repose, without desire, consciousness, or suffering.

7. F. M. Cornford, *Principium Sapientiae: A Study of the Origins of Greek Philosophical Thought* (New York: Harper Torchbooks, 1965), 98–99.

8. Carl Levenson and Jonathan Westphal, *Reality* (Indianapolis, IN: Hackett Publishing, 1994).

9. "The Walrus and the Carpenter," *Lewis Carroll: The Complete Illustrated Works,* Edward Guiliano, ed. (New York: Gramercy Books, 1995), 117.

10. C. S. Lewis, *The Great Divorce* (New York: Touchstone Books, 1996).

11. Sir Russell Brain, *The Nature of Experience* (London, UK: Oxford University Press, 1959).

CHAPTER 15

1. The ultimate "out of sight," of course, is death, and, once dead, a memorial service is held to make the forgetting clean. The horror of ghost stories draws on a feeling of guilt since, after a period, the living do not really want the dead back. See Yi-Fu Tuan, *Landscapes of Fear* (New York: Pantheon Books, 1979), 113–29.

2. Francisco J. Ayala, in his review of Michael Ruse, "Monad to Man," *Science*, Vol. 275 (January 24, 1997): 495.

3. Lynn Hunt, *Inventing Human Rights: A History* (New York: W. W. Norton, 2007).

4. Roger Chartier, *The Cultural Origins of the French Revolution* (Durham, NC: Duke University Press, 1991), 68–69.

CHAPTER 16

1. All biblical quotations come from the authoritative but rare edition, *The Holy Bible: Authorized or King James version containing the Old and New Testaments* (Philadelphia: Universal Book and Bible House, n.d.).

2. Lionel Trilling, *Beyond Culture* (New York: Harvest/HBJ Book, 1965), 56.

3. Staffan B. Linder, *The Harried Leisure Class* (New York: Columbia University Press, 1970).

4. Sophocles, *Oedipus at Colonus* (406 BCE), lines 1224–26.

5. Gareth B. Matthew, *Philosophy and the Young Child* (Cambridge, MA: Harvard University Press, 1980), 7.

6. Myra Bluebond-Langner, *The Private Worlds of Dying Children* (Princeton, NJ: Princeton University Press, 1978), 191.

CHAPTER 17

1. Georgina Ferry, "As Old as You Feel," *Oxford Today*, Vol.7, No. 1 (1994): 18.

2. M. I. Finley, *The World of Odysseus* (Harmondsworth, Middlesex, UK: Penguin Books, 1979), 101–2.

3. Yi-Fu Tuan, "Progress and Anxiety," in Robert Sack, ed., *Progress: Geographical Essays* (Baltimore, MD: The Johns Hopkins University Press, in association with the Center for American Places, 2002), 78–96.

CHAPTER 18

1. David Cannadine and Simon Price, ed., *Rituals of Royalty: Power and Ceremonial in* Traditional Societies (Cambridge, UK: Cambridge University Press, 1987), 143.

2. Richard Ellman, *Oscar Wilde* (New York: Vintage Books, 1988), 121.

3. W. H. Lewis, *The Splendid Century: Some Aspects of French Life in the Reign of Louis XIV* (London, UK: Eyre & Spottswoode, 1953; New York: Quill Paperback Edition, 1978), 202.

4. Among Western scholars, Herbert Fingarette most forcefully emphasizes this point. See the chapter, "Human Community as Holy Rite," in *Confucius—The Secular As Sacred* (New York: Harper Torchbooks, 1972), 1–17.

5. A compelling picture of the transfer of culture from one generation to the next can be found in the award-winning book by Gina J. Grillo, *Between Cultures: Children of Immigrants in America* (Santa Fe and Staunton, VA: The Center for American Places, in association with Columbia College Chicago, 2004). Grillo's focus is on Chicago at the turn of the twenty-first century.

6. This is certainly Leo Tolstoy's view. See his last major work, *A Calendar of Wisdom: Daily Thoughts to Nourish the Soul,* translated by Peter Sekirin. (New York: Charles Scribner's Sons, 1997; compiled by Tolstoy between 1903 and then originally published in Russian in 1910).

7. A striking example is the success of the Simon Bolivar Youth Orchestra of Venezuela on the international stage. The young players come from mixed backgrounds, including gang-ridden slums of Caracas. In 2007, the orchestra,

under the leadership of Gustavo Dudamel (b. 1981; only twenty-six years old at the time) played Beethoven's *Symphony No. 3*, the *Eroica Symphony* (1805), in Bonn, Germany, to rave acclaim. These young musicians are immersed in the classical musical culture of Europe. They are professionals in the highest degree. Does this mean a dilution of their commitment to their own culture—to Venezuelan music? Not at all. Quite the opposite. Their success in the classical repertoire makes them more—not less—proud of their own culture and musical tradition.

8. Walter Goldschmidt, *Comparative Functionalism* (Berkeley: University of California Press, 1966), 134.

9. There are notable exceptions. See Arnold R. Alanen and Robert Z. Melnick, eds., *Preserving Cultural Landscapes in America* (Baltimore, MD: The Johns Hopkins University Press, in association with the Center for American Places, 2000).

10. Robert Sack, *A Geographical Guide to the Real and the Good* (New York: Routledge, in association with the Center for American Places, 2003).

11. Victor Lowe, *Alfred North Whitehead: The Man and His Work, Volume II, 1910–1947* (Baltimore, MD: The Johns Hopkins University Press, 1990).

12. Martin Buber, *The Writings of Martin Buber* (New York: Meridian Books, 1956), 129.

13. Charles Taylor, *A Secular Age* (Cambridge, MA: Harvard University Press, 2007), 695–99.

CHAPTER 19

1. As quoted in Josef Pieper, *Death and Immortality* (South Bend, IN: St. Augustine's Press, 1969), 5.

Index

———

About the Author

————————

Y I-FU TUAN was born in Tiajin, China, in 1930, attended grade schools in China, Australia, and Philippines, before earning undergraduate and graduate degrees in geography, respectively, at Oxford University and the University of California at Berkeley. For may years he taught at the University of Minnesota, and from 1984 until his official retirement in 1998 he held two endowed chairs at the University of Wisconsin-Madison as the John K. Wright Professor of Geography and the Vilas Research Professor of Geography. Professor Tuan is a Fellow of both the British Academy and American Academy of Arts and Sciences, was a founding board member of the Center for American Places, and in 2012 received the prestigious Vautrin Lud International Geography Prize, the highest award given in the field of geography and named after the French scholar who is credited with naming the New World "America" after the Florentine navigator Amerigo Vespucci (1454–1512). Professor Tuan's books include *Humanist Geography: An Individual's Search for Meaning* (2012), *Religion: From Place to Placelessness*, with Martha A. Strawn (2009), *Human Goodness* (2008), *Coming Home to China* (2007), *Place, Art, and Self* (2004), *Dear Colleague: Common and Uncommon Observations* (2002), *Who Am I? An Autobiography of Emotion, Mind, and Spirit* (1999), *Cosmos and Earth: A Cosmopolite's Viewpoint* (1999), *Escapism* (1998), *Passing Strange and Wonderful: Aesthetics, Nature, and Culture* (1993), *Morality and Imagination: Paradoxes of Progress* (1989), *The Good Life* (1986), *Dominance and Affection: The Making of Pets* (1984), *Segmented Worlds and Self: Group Life and Individual Consciousness* (1982), *Landscapes of Fear* (1979; 2012), *Space and Place: The Perspective of Experience* (1977), *Topophilia: A Study of Environmental Perception, Attitudes, and Values* (1974; 1990), *Man and Nature* (1971), *China* (1969), which was reprinted in 2008 under the title: *A Historical Geography of China*, and *The Hydrologic Cycle and the Wisdom of God: A Theme in Geoteleogy (1968)*. Professor Tuan continues to write from his home in Madison, Wisconsin.

About the Book

Humanist Geography: An Individual's Search for Meaning was brought to publication in an edition of 1,500 softcover copies. The text was set in Minion with Avenir display, the paper is Huron Matte, 70lb weight, and the book was professionally printed and bound in United States of America. The photographs *Untitled # 222–04* (on pages ii–iii) and *Untitled #1132–04* (on page v) are from the *On the Beach* series by Richard Misrach, and they appear courtesy of the artist, Fraenkel Gallery, of San Francisco, Pace-MacGill Gallery, of New York City, and Marc Selwyn Fine Arts, of Los Angeles.

Editor and Publisher: George F. Thompson
Editorial Assistants: Carmen Rose Shenk and Stephanie Lichner
Indexer: Alison Drew Hunt
Book Design and Production: David Skolkin

The publisher extends special thanks to Richard Misrach, for the use of his two photographs, as well as those who greatly assisted in the editorial development, production, and promotion of this book: J. Nicholas Entrikin, Randall B. Jones, Melanie McCalmont, Dominic Pacyga, John Perry, Morgan Pfaelzer, Jared Shlaes, Paul F. Starrs, Denis Wood, and our colleagues at the University of Wisconsin Press.

Published in 2012. First Edition.
Printed in the United States of America on acid-free paper.

George F. Thompson Publishing, L.L.C.
217 Oak Ridge Circle
Staunton, Virginia 24401-3511, U.S.A.
www.gftbooks.com

20 19 18 17 16 15 14 13 12   1 2 3 4 5

The Library of Congress Control Number is 2012931439.

ISBN: 978–0–9834978–1–3